hamlyn cookery club

Easy
vegetarian

hamlyn cookery club

Easy
vegetarian

First published in 1999 by Hamlyn
an imprint of Octopus Publishing Group
2–4 Heron Quays
London E14 4JP

British Library Cataloguing-in-Publication Data
A catalogue record for this book is available from the
British Library.

ISBN 0 600 59906 X

Printed in China

Publishing Director: Laura Bamford
Copy Editor: Isobel Holland
Creative Director: Keith Martin
Design Manager: Bryan Dunn
Designer: Ginny Zeal
Jacket Photography: Sean Myers
Picture Researchers: Stevie Moe and Christine Junemann
Production Controller: Katherine Hockley

Notes

1 Both metric and imperial measurements have been given in
all recipes. Use one set of measurements only and not a
mixture of both.

2 Standard level spoon measurements are used in all recipes.
1 tablespoon = one 15 ml spoon
1 teaspoon = one 5 ml spoon

3 Eggs should be medium unless otherwise stated.

4 Milk should be full fat unless otherwise stated.

5 Fresh herbs should be used unless otherwise stated.
If unavailable use dried herbs as an alternative but halve the
quantities stated.

6 Pepper should be freshly ground black pepper unless
otherwise stated.

7 Ovens should be preheated to the specified temperature
– if using a fan-assisted oven, follow the manufacturer's
instructions for adjusting the time and temperature.

8 Measurements for canned food have been given as a
standard metric equivalent.

Contents

Introduction

Vegetarian dishes are featuring with increasing frequency on dinner tables, in lunch boxes and on trays in front of the television, not only because there are more 'full-time' vegetarians, but also because people have realized that vegetarian dishes are not just for vegetarians. There are some delicious, easy-to-cook recipes that are a far cry from the old-fashioned nut-loaf and fatty food image.

Becoming a Vegetarian

There is an ever-growing number of vegetarians. Some people give up eating meat on moral or compassionate grounds, but probably the most common reason is one of health. There are some who take to vegetarianism in the hope of losing weight. Whilst eating a balanced vegetarian diet certainly can help towards weight loss through an increased intake of unrefined carbohydrate foods, vegetables and fruits and the associated reduction of fat, if flesh foods are replaced by fat-rich foods a slimmer figure will not result. Not only does this mean being careful about the amount of pastries, cakes and sweets that are eaten, but also dairy foods that are high in fat, such as hard cheeses, butter and eggs.

A Well-balanced Diet

Following a well-balanced vegetarian diet is, without doubt, a healthy way of eating. It leads, on average, to a 20% lower blood cholesterol level and a 30% lower cancer rate than when meat is eaten. There is also less incidence of heart disease, kidney stones, diabetes, diverticulitis, piles, osteoporosis, rheumatoid arthritis, gout and dental decay.

Degrees of Vegetarianism

Even if not a vegetarian yourself, you might well have at least one vegetarian in the family and have several friends who are vegetarians. If cooking for someone who says that they are a vegetarian, it is useful to clarify exactly what form of vegetarianism they practice because there are a number of different degrees of vegetarianism. Lacto-ovo vegetarians, who are in the majority, eat eggs and milk products such as cheese, yogurt, butter and cream. Lacto-vegetarians eat milk products but not eggs while vegans will not eat any product that is of animal origin, only plant foods. A half-way house towards vegetarianism is the category known as demi-vegetarianism because its adherents eschew red meat but eat fish, and sometimes poultry.

Products to Avoid

Particular pitfalls to watch out for are gelatine, which is an animal derivative (agar-agar, from seaweed, is a suitable alternative), and stock. Most cheeses are made using rennet from an animal source, but there is a growing number that aren't so look for words such as 'Suitable for vegetarians' or the 'V' symbol on the label. This applies to other packaged prepared 'convenience' products as well.

Planning to become Vegetarian

When planning to becoming a vegetarian, it is a good idea to do so gradually, to accustom your digestive system to the change in diet. Increase the amount of plant foods on the plate and reduce the size of meat, poultry and fish portions, and omit them all together from two, then three then four days a week, and so on. Replace animal protein foods with plant foods that are high in protein, such as dried beans, peas and lentils rather than cheese and eggs. Fill up with wholemeal bread, rice and other grains, pasta, vegetables and fruits. Cook composite, one-pot dishes such as risottos, paella; curries, main course salads and stir-fries, and make full use of herbs, spices, well-flavoured home-made vegetable stock (there is a simple recipe on page 10) and other virtually calorie-free flavourings to add interest and variety to meals.

Soups, Starters and Snacks

Spinach Soup

750 g (1½ lb) fresh spinach, washed
    thoroughly and stalks removed
25 g (1 oz) butter
1 small onion, finely chopped
25 g (1 oz) plain flour
600 ml (1 pint) vegetable stock
about 300 ml (½ pint) milk
freshly grated nutmeg
salt and pepper
about 2 tablespoons natural yogurt
4 lemon slices (optional)

Cook the spinach without water in a covered pan for 6–8 minutes, then turn into a bowl.

Rinse out the pan and melt the butter in it. Add the chopped onion, fry gently without browning for 5 minutes, then add the flour. Cook for 3 minutes, then pour in the stock. Stir well, bring to the boil and simmer for 3–4 minutes.

Cool slightly, then pour into a blender or food processor, add the spinach and blend until smooth.

Pour back into the pan and stir in sufficient milk to give a pouring consistency. Add nutmeg and salt and pepper to taste. Reheat.

Swirl yogurt into each bowl and garnish with a lemon slice, if liked.

Serves 4

Carrot and Lentil Soup

25 g (1 oz) butter
1 onion, chopped
1 garlic clove, crushed (optional)
2 carrots, about 125 g (4 oz),
    chopped
2 celery sticks, chopped
150 g (5 oz) red lentils, washed and
    drained
1 litre (1¾ pints) vegetable stock
2 teaspoons lemon juice
2 tablespoons chopped parsley
about 150 ml (¼ pint) milk
salt and pepper
Croûtons:
oil, for shallow frying
4 slices wholemeal bread, crusts
    removed and cut into 1 cm (½ inch)
    cubes

Melt the butter in a large pan and fry the onion and garlic, if using, for about 5 minutes until they are soft but not brown.

Add the carrots, celery and lentils and stir around in the butter for a few minutes. Pour in the stock, half-cover the pan and simmer very gently for about 40 minutes, stirring the soup occasionally.

Purée the soup in a blender or food processor, or press through a sieve. Pour back into the saucepan and season to taste with salt and pepper. Add the lemon juice and parsley and thin the soup with milk to the consistency you prefer. Simmer gently to reheat.

To make the croûtons, heat a little oil in a frying pan and fry the bread cubes in 2 batches until golden brown. Drain on kitchen paper.

Serve the soup piping hot in individual bowls, sprinkling with the croûtons at the last moment.

Serves 4

right: spinach soup,
carrot and lentil soup

Homemade Vegetable Stock

Homemade stock makes all the difference to vegetarian recipes. Keep the salt to a minimum and never add green leafy vegetables such as cabbage as they spoil the background flavour. Brown the vegetables well at the start and the stock will be a good golden colour and the flavour rich and full.

1 tablespoon vegetable oil

2 onions, quartered

4 large carrots, about 500 g (1 lb), cut into chunks

3 celery sticks, cut into chunks

1 teaspoon tomato purée

6 black peppercorns

1 teaspoon salt

2.5 litres (4 pints) water

Heat half the oil in a very large saucepan with a lid and fry the onions until quite dark brown. Remove and reserve. Add the remaining oil and brown the carrots. Remove and reserve, then brown the celery.

Put all the vegetables back into the pan and add the tomato purée, peppercorns, salt and water.

Bring to the boil, stirring at first, so that the colour from the bottom of the pan is mixed into the stock. Cover and simmer on the lowest possible heat for about 2 hours.

Strain the stock and leave to cool.

Makes about 1.8 litres (3 pints)

Chinese Bean Sprout Soup

1 litre (1¾ pints) vegetable stock

1 onion, quartered

2 carrots, quartered

4 spring onions, thinly sliced

250 g (8 oz) fresh bean sprouts

2 tablespoons soy sauce

2 tablespoons dry sherry

salt and pepper

2 large radishes, sliced and quartered, to garnish

Put the stock in a pan with the onion and carrots, bring to the boil, cover and simmer for 20 minutes.

Strain the stock thoroughly and discard all the vegetables.

Return the stock to the pan, add the thinly sliced spring onions and bean sprouts and season with salt and pepper. Bring to the boil and simmer gently for 2–3 minutes.

Stir in the soy sauce and sherry, then taste and adjust the seasoning if necessary.

Serve the soup in individual bowls and garnish each serving with quartered radish slices.

Serves 4

above: Chinese bean sprout soup, gingered pumpkin soup
right: almond soup

Gingered Pumpkin Soup

1 kg (2 lb) slice of pumpkin,
   peeled, deseeded and roughly
   chopped
1 piece fresh root ginger,
   peeled
1 tablespoon sunflower oil
1 large onion, chopped
2 teaspoons ground ginger
1 teaspoon ground turmeric
2 large, ripe tomatoes, skinned
   and chopped
2 teaspoons soft light
   brown sugar
¼ teaspoon grated nutmeg
strip thinly-pared orange rind
600 ml (1 pint) vegetable stock
300 ml (½ pint) natural yogurt
salt and pepper
To garnish:
2 tablespoons chopped parsley
6 tablespoons pumpkin seeds

Put the pumpkin into a pan with
the piece of ginger and cover it
with water. Bring to the boil,
cover the pan and simmer for
15 minutes, until the pumpkin is
tender. Drain and reserve the
pumpkin and discard the ginger.

Heat the oil in the pan and fry
the onion over a moderate heat
for 2 minutes. Stir in the ground
ginger and turmeric, then cook
gently for 1 minute.

Add the pumpkin, tomatoes,
sugar, nutmeg, orange rind and
stock and bring to the boil. Cover

and simmer for 10 minutes. Cool
slightly. Discard the orange rind.

Purée the pumpkin mixture in
a blender or press through a
sieve, then return the purée to
the pan. Season with salt and
pepper and stir in the yogurt.
Heat gently. Taste and adjust the
seasoning if necessary.

Garnish each serving with the
parsley and pumpkin seeds.

Serves 6

Almond Soup

1 litre (1¾ pints) vegetable
   stock
2 celery sticks, chopped
1 small onion, quartered
1 bouquet garni
2 bay leaves
1 mace blade
250 g (8 oz) ground almonds
100 ml (3½ fl oz) sweet sherry

125 ml (4 fl oz) natural yogurt
salt and white pepper
40 g (1½ oz) flaked almonds,
   toasted, to garnish

Put the stock into a pan, add the
celery, onion, bouquet garni, bay
leaves and mace and season with
salt and white pepper.

Bring slowly to the boil, with
the pan uncovered, and skim off
any foam from the top. Cover the
pan and simmer gently for about
25 minutes.

Strain the stock, discarding the
flavourings, and return it to the
pan.

Stir in the ground almonds,
add the sherry, cover the pan and
simmer for 20 minutes.

Stir in the yogurt and heat
through gently. Taste and adjust
the seasoning if necessary.

Scatter the soup with the
toasted almonds. Serve hot.

Serves 4

Red Pepper Soup

1 tablespoon sunflower oil

1 large onion, chopped

2 garlic cloves, finely chopped

2 tablespoons sherry

3 large red peppers, deseeded, cored
   and cut into strips

1 potato, diced

2 tablespoons tomato purée

2 large tomatoes, skinned and sliced

1 litre (1¾ pints) vegetable stock, hot

1 bay leaf

1 bouquet garni

salt and pepper

To garnish:

2 tablespoons natural yogurt

parsley or chervil sprigs

Heat the oil in a large pan and fry the onion over a moderate heat for 4–5 minutes, stirring once or twice. Stir in the garlic, sherry, peppers, potato, tomato purée and tomatoes and add the stock with the bay leaf, bouquet garni and salt and pepper.

Bring to the boil, cover the pan and simmer for 30 minutes.

With a slotted spoon, remove 2 spoonfuls of peppers and set them aside. Discard the bay leaf and bouquet garni and purée the soup in a blender or pass through a sieve.

Return the soup to the pan, stir in the peppers, taste and adjust the seasoning and heat gently.

Serve hot, garnished with swirls of yogurt and chervil or parsley sprigs.

Serves 4–6

Artichoke Soup

25 g (1 oz) butter

1 small onion, sliced

500 g (1 lb) Jerusalem
   artichokes, sliced

600 ml (1 pint) milk

300 ml (½ pint) vegetable stock

salt and pepper

snipped chives, to garnish (optional)

Melt the butter in a large pan and fry the onion gently without browning for about 5 minutes.

Add the artichokes, cover and cook for another 5 minutes so that the artichokes absorb the butter.

Add salt and pepper to taste, then pour in the milk and stock. Bring to the boil and simmer gently, half-covered, for about 20 minutes, until the artichokes are tender.

Blend in a liquidizer or food processor until smooth or push the soup through a sieve. Return the soup to the pan and reheat gently.

Taste and adjust the seasoning. Serve piping hot, sprinkled with chives, if using, and Sesame Croûtons (see right).

Serves 4

left: red pepper soup
right: artichoke soup,
leek and potato soup

Sesame Croûtons

4 slices brown bread, crusts removed
1 egg, beaten
sesame seeds
oil, for shallow-frying
salt and pepper

Dip each slice of bread into the beaten egg seasoned with salt and pepper and then into the sesame seeds, coating both sides well. Cut the dipped slices into squares, then cut each square into 2 triangles. Fry in shallow hot oil for about 30 seconds. Lift out with a slotted spoon and drain on kitchen paper.

Makes 32

Leek and Potato Soup

1 tablespoon vegetable oil
15 g (½ oz) butter
1 small onion, thinly sliced
1 large leek, about 250 g (8 oz), sliced
375 g (12 oz) potatoes, cut into 5 mm (¼ inch) cubes
900 ml (1½ pints) vegetable stock
1 bay leaf
salt and pepper
2 tablespoons chopped parsley

Heat the oil and butter in a large pan and gently fry the onion for 3–4 minutes without browning.

Add the leek and potatoes, stir well, then cover the pan and leave over a low heat for a few minutes until the butter and oil are absorbed into the vegetables.

Pour in the vegetable stock and add a little salt, plenty of pepper and the bay leaf.

Cover the pan again, bring to the boil and simmer gently for about 15 minutes. Take care not to overcook.

Test to make sure the potato is tender, then taste and adjust the seasoning and remove the bay leaf.

Stir in the chopped parsley and serve piping hot.

Serves 4

Light Vegetable Soup

25 g (1 oz) butter
1 small onion, finely chopped
175 g (6 oz) carrots, cut into narrow
   matchstick strips
3 celery sticks, finely sliced
1 teaspoon cornflour
900 ml (1½ pints) vegetable stock
1 teaspoon tomato purée
2 tablespoons chopped parsley
celery leaves, to garnish
Omelette:
2 eggs
15 g (½ oz) butter
salt and pepper

Melt the butter in a large pan and
fry the onion gently without
browning for about 5 minutes.

Add the carrots and celery, cover
and cook gently for a few more
minutes until the butter is absorbed.

Stir in the cornflour, then add the
stock and tomato purée. Bring to
the boil, half-cover the pan and
simmer for about 20 minutes.

Make the omelette. Beat the eggs
with salt and pepper. Melt the
butter in a small frying pan, add the
eggs and fry until set and pale brown
underneath. Turn over and brown
the other side. Remove from the
pan and cut into 1 cm (½ inch) dice.

Stir the parsley into the soup and
serve garnished with a few pieces of
the omelette and celery leaves.

Serves 4

Mushroom and Hazelnut Soup

25 g (1 oz) butter
375 g (12 oz) mushrooms, sliced
25 g (1 oz) ground hazelnuts
450 ml (¾ pint) vegetable stock
450 ml (¾ pint) milk
¼ teaspoon grated nutmeg
3 tablespoons single cream
salt and pepper

Melt the butter in a large pan, add
the mushrooms and stir over a
medium heat for 2–3 minutes until
the juices run. Put the lid on the
pan and simmer the mushrooms
gently in the juices for 5 minutes.
Take out 2 tablespoons of the
mushrooms and reserve them for
garnishing later.

Stir in the hazelnuts, then add the
stock, milk, nutmeg, salt and
pepper. Cover the pan and simmer
gently for 10 minutes.

Purée the soup in a liquidizer or
food processor, or press through a
sieve. Return to the rinsed pan, stir
in the cream and the reserved
cooked mushrooms and gently
reheat until the soup is piping hot
but not boiling.

Check and adjust the seasoning if
necessary. Serve immediately.

Serves 4

Watercress Soup

25 g (1 oz) butter
1 onion, finely chopped
3 spring onions, sliced
3 bunches watercress, trimmed and
   chopped
25 g (1 oz) wholemeal flour
1 litre (1¾ pints) vegetable stock
150 ml (¼ pint) natural yogurt
salt and pepper
small watercress sprigs, to garnish

Melt the butter in a large pan and
fry the onion, spring onions and
watercress over a low heat for 10
minutes, stirring frequently.

Remove from the heat, add the
flour and stir until the flour has
absorbed the fat. Return the pan to
the heat, increase to moderate and
gradually pour on the stock, stirring
constantly. Season with salt and
pepper, bring to the boil and cover
the pan. Simmer for 15 minutes.

Cool slightly, then purée in a
blender or press through a sieve.

Return the puréed soup to the
pan, stir in the yogurt, then taste
and adjust the seasoning if
necessary. Reheat gently.

Serve the soup hot, garnished
with the watercress sprigs.

Serves 6

*right: light vegetable soup,
mushroom and hazelnut soup*

Celeriac and Orange Soup

1 celeriac, about 375 g (12 oz), roughly chopped

1 potato, roughly chopped

2 carrots, sliced

1 litre (1¾ pints) vegetable stock

thinly pared rind of ½ orange

1 teaspoon grated orange rind

1 tablespoon orange juice

6 tablespoons natural yogurt

salt and pepper

Put the celeriac, potato and carrots into a pan with the stock and bring to the boil. Cover the pan and simmer for 30 minutes, or until all the vegetables are soft.

Cut the orange rind into very thin matchstick strips. Place them in a saucepan with a little boiling water and boil for 10 minutes, then drain. Reserve for the garnish.

Cool the vegetables and stock slightly, then purée in a blender or press through a sieve.

Return to the pan, add the grated orange rind and juice and season with salt and pepper. Bring back to the boil and simmer for 5 minutes.

To serve, pour the soup into individual dishes or bowls, swirl 1 tablespoon yogurt on to each portion and garnish with the reserved strips of orange rind.

Serves 6

below: celeriac and orange soup, curried cauliflower soup variation
right: *sweetcorn soup*

Curried Cauliflower Soup

1 tablespoon sunflower oil

1 onion, sliced

2 teaspoons curry powder
  (or to taste)

1 small cauliflower, roughly
  chopped

900 ml (1½ pints) vegetable stock

salt and pepper

4 tablespoons sunflower seeds,
  to garnish

Heat the oil in a large pan and fry the onion over a moderate heat for 2 minutes. Stir in the curry powder and cook for 1 minute.

Add the cauliflower and stock, season with salt and pepper and bring to the boil. Cover the pan and simmer for 20 minutes.

Cool slightly, then purée the vegetables and stock in a blender or press through a sieve.

Return to the pan. Taste and adjust the seasoning if necessary and reheat. Serve garnished with the sunflower seeds.

Serves 4

Variation:

To add an interesting texture to the soup, cut off a few very small cauliflower florets before blending and set them aside. Add them to the purée when reheating the soup.

Sweetcorn Soup

1.5 litres (2½ pints) vegetable stock

1 onion, thinly sliced

1 leek, white part only, thinly sliced

3 potatoes, diced

150 ml (¼ pint) milk or buttermilk

375 g (12 oz) sweetcorn kernels

175 g (6 oz) can baby sweetcorn
  (optional)

2 tablespoons chopped parsley

salt and pepper

Put the stock into a large pan with the onion, leek and potatoes, season with salt and pepper and bring to the boil. Cover the pan and simmer for 20 minutes. Cool slightly, then purée in a blender or press through a sieve.

Return the purée to the pan and stir in the milk or buttermilk. Add the corn kernels and baby sweetcorn (if using), and heat gently.

Taste and adjust the seasoning. Stir in the parsley. Serve hot.

Serves 6–8

Cheese Dip

25 g (1 oz) butter
175 g (6 oz) low fat soft cheese
1 teaspoon Dijon mustard
1 teaspoon anchovy paste
1 teaspoon paprika, plus extra for
  garnish
1 tablespoon chopped gherkin
1 tablespoon chopped capers
1 teaspoon finely snipped chives, plus
  extra for garnish
pepper

Beat the butter until it is soft. Beat in the cheese, mustard, anchovy paste and paprika and beat until the mixture is smooth. Stir in the gherkin, capers and chives and season with pepper.

Spoon the dip into a serving bowl and sprinkle on a little paprika and a few chopped chives to garnish.

Serves 4–6

Celery Dip

175 g (6 oz) low fat soft cheese
2 tablespoons natural yogurt
3 celery sticks, finely chopped
2 tablespoons chopped celery leaves
1 teaspoon celery seeds
salt and pepper
chopped celery leaves, to garnish

Beat the cheese and yogurt and stir in the finely chopped celery sticks, leaves and seeds. Season to taste with salt and pepper.

Spoon the dip into a serving bowl and garnish with the celery leaves.

Serves 4

above: celery dip, butter bean dip
right: cheese dip
far right: nut stuffed tomatoes

Butter Bean Dip

125 g (4 oz) dried butter beans,
  soaked overnight and drained
4 tablespoons sunflower or
  olive oil
2 garlic cloves, crushed
2 tablespoons cider vinegar
2 tablespoons chopped parsley
salt and pepper
chopped parsley, to garnish

Cook the beans in boiling unsalted water for 1 hour until tender. Drain them, reserving the liquid, rinse in running cold water and drain again.

Purée the beans in a blender with the oil, garlic, cider vinegar and 3 tablespoons of the reserved liquid.

Stir in the parsley and season with salt and pepper. Garnish with the chopped parsley.

Serves 4

Nut Stuffed Tomatoes

2 large beefsteak tomatoes
salt and pepper
Stuffing:
2 tablespoons vegetable oil
75 g (3 oz) button mushrooms, finely
   chopped
60 g (2½ oz) brown rice, cooked
25 g (1 oz) Brazil nuts, coarsely
   chopped
25 g (1 oz) currants
1 teaspoon chopped fresh basil or
   ½ teaspoon dried basil
To garnish:
4 teaspoons soured cream
watercress sprigs

Cut the tomatoes in half and scoop
out the pulp. Sprinkle the shells
with salt and place in a baking dish.

To make the stuffing, heat the oil
in a small pan and gently fry the
mushrooms for 5 minutes. Stir in
the cooked rice, nuts, currants and
basil. Add a little salt and plenty of
pepper to taste.

Spoon the stuffing into the
tomato halves.

Cover the dish with foil to keep
the stuffing moist and bake in a
preheated oven, 180°C (350°F), Gas
Mark 4, for 20 minutes.

Remove from the oven, top each
stuffed tomato with a spoonful of
soured cream and watercress sprigs.
Serve piping hot.

Serves 2

Spicy Tomato Chickpeas

A warming light supper for two, which
is quickly prepared and cooked. Serve
with plain brown rice and perhaps a
bowl of crunchy raw fennel.

2 teaspoons vegetable oil
1 onion, sliced
½ teaspoon garam masala
½ teaspoon ground cumin
¼ teaspoon ground chilli
dash of Tabasco sauce
400 g (13 oz) can tomatoes
1 teaspoon tomato purée
2 teaspoons sugar
1 green pepper, cored, deseeded and
   diced
425 g (14 oz) can chickpeas
salt and pepper

Heat the oil and fry the onion
gently for 5 minutes. Stir in the
garam masala, cumin, chilli and
Tabasco sauce.

Pour in the tomatoes with their
juice, tomato purée, sugar, salt and
pepper. Simmer gently, uncovered,
for about 4 minutes, then add the
green pepper.

Continue simmering for a further
3–4 minutes until the sauce is
smooth and thick.

Drain the chickpeas and reserve
4 tablespoons of liquid. Stir the
chickpeas and reserved liquid into
the sauce and cook gently for
8–10 minutes to heat the chickpeas,
stirring from time to time.

Serve piping hot.

Serves 2

Avocado and Stilton Toasts

4 slices wholemeal bread
15 g (½ oz) butter
1 large ripe avocado
1 tablespoon lemon juice
pepper
75 g (3 oz) blue Stilton cheese
To garnish:
8 small lettuce leaves
watercress sprigs

Place the wholemeal bread under a preheated hot grill and toast on 1 side. Lightly butter the untoasted side. Keep warm.

Peel and halve the avocado, removing the stone. Cut into quarters, then cut each quarter into 4 slices.

Arrange the slices of avocado on the buttered side of each piece of toast and sprinkle with lemon juice and pepper.

Cut the cheese into 4 thin slices and lay 1 slice over the avocado slices on each piece of toast.

Reduce the grill to medium and grill the toasts lightly until the cheese is melted.

Serve immediately garnished with the lettuce and watercress sprigs.

Serves 4

Cheese Granary Toasts

4 tablespoons milk
25 g (1 oz) butter
2 teaspoons malt vinegar
pepper
large pinch of cayenne pepper
½ teaspoon made English mustard
250 g (8 oz) mature Cheddar cheese, grated
salt (optional)
8–12 slices granary bread
To garnish:
mustard and cress
paprika

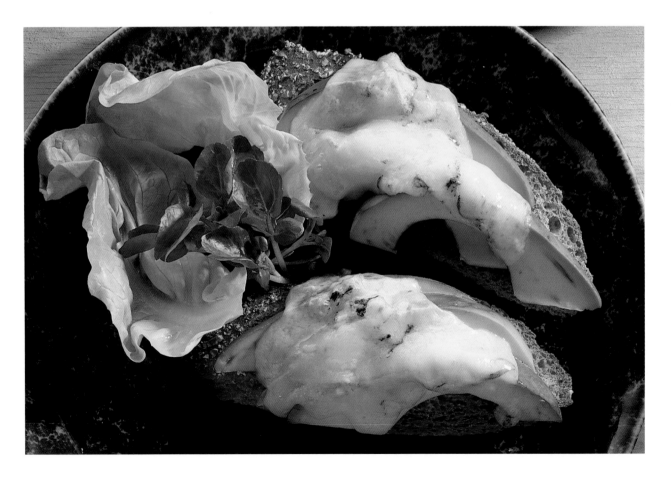

Put the milk, butter, vinegar, pepper, cayenne and mustard into a pan.

Bring slowly to the boil, then take off the heat and add the grated cheese immediately and all at once.

Beat thoroughly for 1 minute until the mixture is light and creamy. Taste and add a little salt if necessary. The cheese topping is now ready to spread.

Toast the bread on 1 side only. Spread the untoasted side thickly with the topping and put back under the grill for 3–4 minutes until the topping is golden brown.

Cut in half and serve immediately garnished with mustard and cress and a sprinkling of paprika.

Makes 8–12

Variation:
For a different taste and texture, stir 25 g (1 oz) chopped salted peanuts into the mixture before spreading on to the bread (but do not add any salt to the mixture).

left: avocado and Stilton toasts
right: raw winter vegetables with skordalia

Raw Winter Vegetables with Skordalia

Serve this Greek dip with some or all of the suggested raw vegetables. Remember that vegetables quickly lose their vitamins once cut, so choose very fresh crisp vegetables and prepare them only 1–2 hours before serving.

Dip:
300 ml (½ pint) mayonnaise
25 g (1 oz) fresh wholemeal
    breadcrumbs
25 g (1 oz) ground almonds
2 garlic cloves, crushed
    (or more, to taste)
squeeze of lemon juice
2 tablespoons sesame seeds,
    toasted
3 tablespoons chopped parsley
2–4 tablespoons natural yogurt
    (optional)
salt and pepper
Vegetables:
about 175 g (6 oz) each of: celeriac,
    carrot, white cabbage, red
    cabbage, trimmed broccoli,
    trimmed cauliflower, onions, celery

To make the dip, put the mayonnaise into a bowl and then stir in the breadcrumbs and almonds. Add the garlic, salt, pepper and lemon juice.

Now stir in the sesame seeds and parsley. If the mixture seems a little stiff, add natural yogurt to give a

softer consistency. Taste and adjust the seasoning. Cover and set aside while preparing the vegetables.

Grate the celeriac and carrot, shred the white and red cabbage and thinly slice the broccoli, cauliflower, onions and celery.

Serve clusters of the vegetables on a large platter or in small separate dishes, with the dip in the centre.

Serves 4

Potato Jackets

5 large potatoes, scrubbed and dried
Dip:
150 ml (¼ pint) soured cream
1 teaspoon snipped chives
salt and pepper
vegetable oil, for frying

Prick the potatoes with a fork and bake in a preheated oven, 190°C (375°F), Gas Mark 5, for about 1¼ hours until tender; really large potatoes will take about 30 minutes longer to cook.

Meanwhile, make the dip. Mix the soured cream with the chives and salt and pepper to taste. Spoon into a bowl, cover and leave to chill in the refrigerator.

When the potatoes are cooked, cool for a few minutes, then cut each one lengthways into 4.

Using a teaspoon scoop out most of the potato leaving just a thin layer next to the skin.

Pour vegetable oil into a small pan to a depth of 7 cm (3 inches). There is no need to use a large deep frying pan.

Heat the oil in the pan to 180–190°C (350–375°F) or until a cube of bread browns in 30 seconds.

Fry 4–5 potato skins at a time for about 2 minutes until brown and crisp. Lift from the oil with a slotted spoon and drain on kitchen paper. Keep the potato skins hot in the oven while the remaining skins are being cooked.

Either sprinkle the skins lightly with salt or provide salt for guests to help themselves. Serve with the chilled dip.

Serves 4

above: potato jackets, smoked cheese and nut salad
right: mushroom pâté

Mushroom Pâté

A useful vegetarian spread. Tasty with chopped watercress as a sandwich filling, or served with warm granary bread and butter.

25 g (1 oz) butter
2 shallots or small onions, finely sliced
1 garlic clove, crushed (optional)
250 g (8 oz) flat mushrooms, sliced
25 g (1 oz) fresh wholemeal breadcrumbs
125 g (4 oz) cottage cheese
large pinch of ground nutmeg
large pinch of ground mace
50 g (2 oz) butter, melted
salt and pepper
1 tablespoon chopped parsley, to garnish
lemon wedges, to serve

Melt half the butter in a pan with a lid and fry the shallots or onions and garlic gently for 3 minutes. Add the mushrooms, cover the pan and cook for 15 minutes. Remove the lid, turn up the heat and reduce the liquid until the mushrooms are just moist.

Cool slightly, then put the mushrooms with the breadcrumbs, cheese, nutmeg, mace, salt, pepper and melted butter in a blender or food processor and blend together until smooth.

Taste and adjust the seasoning, and spoon the pâté into a small dish. Cover and chill for 1–2 hours in the refrigerator.

Just before serving sprinkle the top of the pâté with parsley. Serve with lemon wedges.

Serves 4

Smoked Cheese and Nut Salad

An unusual colourful starter using radicchio. The same quantities will serve 2–3 as a main meal salad.

1 crisp lettuce, shredded
1 head radicchio, separated into leaves
2 apples
1 tablespoon lemon juice
150 g (5 oz) German smoked cheese, cut into 1 cm (½ inch) cubes
1 bunch watercress, to garnish

Nut dressing:
50 g (2 oz) hazelnuts, coarsely chopped
3 tablespoons hazelnut oil
3 tablespoons sunflower oil
2 tablespoons wine vinegar
pinch of cayenne pepper
½ teaspoon made English mustard
½ teaspoon sugar
salt and pepper

To make the nut dressing, toast the hazelnuts under a preheated medium grill until they are evenly browned. Cool.

Put all the remaining dressing ingredients into a screw-top jar, add the hazelnuts and shake for 1 minute until well mixed.

Arrange the lettuce and radicchio on 6 individual plates. Core the apples and cut into 1 cm (½ inch) cubes, toss in the lemon juice and arrange with the cubes of cheese on top of the salad leaves.

Spoon the nut dressing over the cheese and apple salad just before serving. Garnish with watercress sprigs and serve.

Serves 6

Fennel with Walnuts

Crisp aniseed flavoured fennel smothered in hot walnut dressing is simply delicious and made in minutes.

2 small fennel bulbs, with leaves
Dressing:
4 tablespoons olive oil
1 garlic clove, crushed (optional)
125 g (4 oz) walnuts, chopped
salt and pepper

Slice the fennel into thin, short strips, reserving the feathery leaves. Divide among 4 individual dishes.

Heat the olive oil in a small pan and add the garlic and walnuts. Fry quickly until the walnuts begin to brown. Add salt and pepper, then spoon the dressing over the fennel.

Garnish with the reserved fennel leaves and serve immediately.

Serves 4

Blinis

Blinis are little pancakes; a Russian version of Scotch pancakes. Buckwheat flour gives them a speckled dark colour and a distinct flavour but is not always easy to find, so use wholemeal instead if necessary. Buckwheat flour will absorb less liquid than wholemeal so use slightly under the measure of milk to begin with, adding more if the batter seems too thick.

125 g (4 oz) buckwheat flour
  or plain wholemeal flour
125 g (4 oz) plain white flour
½ teaspoon salt
2 teaspoons easy-blend yeast
1 egg, separated
1 tablespoon vegetable oil
about 300 ml (½ pint) tepid
  milk
To serve:
a selection of toppings (see page 25)
watercress sprigs, to garnish
  (optional)

Put the flours, salt, yeast, egg yolk and oil into a bowl. Pour in the milk and mix to a thick, smooth batter. Cover and leave for 1 hour. The surface of the batter should be puffy and covered with bubbles.

Whisk the egg white and fold into the batter. The mixture is now ready for use.

Lightly oil a griddle or frying pan and put over a steady heat. Drop 2 tablespoons of batter into the pan and cook for 3 minutes until tiny holes appear over the surface. Turn the pancake over and cook the other side for 2 minutes. Cook 3–4 blinis at a time. When ready, keep warm between the layers of a clean tea towel, folded on a plate over boiling water.

To serve, arrange 2–3 warm blinis with 1 or more of the chosen toppings on some warmed plates and garnish each serving with watercress sprigs if liked.

Makes 16–20

Suggested Toppings for Blinis:

- Cottage cheese with radish and cress
- Diced apple and celery mixed with yogurt
- Soured cream with chopped pecan nuts
- Mozzarella cheese with stuffed olives
- Sliced tomatoes with soured cream
- Diced cucumber with natural yogurt

Serves 2

Courgette Fritters with Blue Cheese Dip

Short sticks of celery or small florets of cauliflower may be used for the fritters instead of courgettes and then cooked in the same way.

5 small courgettes, about
   300 g (10 oz)
vegetable oil, for frying
Batter:
125 g (4 oz) wholemeal
   self-raising flour
1 egg
1 tablespoon vegetable oil
2 teaspoons vinegar
150 ml (¼ pint) milk
salt and pepper
Dip:
4 tablespoons mayonnaise
4 tablespoons natural yogurt
50 g (2 oz) Danish Blue cheese,
   crumbled

Trim the courgettes and cut into short sticks about 5 cm (2 inches) long and 5 mm (¼ inch) wide. Dry on kitchen paper.

To make the batter, put the flour, salt, pepper, egg, oil, vinegar and half the milk into a bowl, whisk to a thick paste, then gradually whisk in the rest of the milk.

To make the dip, blend the mayonnaise and yogurt together in a bowl, fold in the cheese and season with plenty of pepper.

Pour enough vegetable oil into a small pan to come to a depth of about 7 cm (3 inches); there is no need to use a large deep-frying pan. Heat the oil to 180–190°C (350–375°F) or until a cube of bread browns in 30 seconds.

Dip each piece of courgette into the batter, allowing any excess to run back into the bowl, and then fry in small batches until puffy and golden (about 3 minutes per batch). Lift out with a slotted spoon, drain on kitchen paper, and keep hot on a serving dish in a preheated oven, 110°C (225°F), Gas Mark ¼, until all the courgettes have been cooked.

Sprinkle the fritters lightly with salt and serve hot with the dip.

Serves 4

*left: fennel with walnuts, blinis
below: courgette fritters with blue cheese dip*

Main Dishes

Vegetable Kebabs with Coriander Rice

2 courgettes
4 button onions or shallots
8 small button mushrooms, trimmed
4 tomatoes, halved, or 8 cherry tomatoes
1 red pepper, cored, deseeded and cut into 5 cm (2 inch) squares
12 small bay leaves
salt and pepper
Marinade:
4 tablespoons sunflower oil
1 tablespoon red wine vinegar
1 tablespoon lemon juice
1 garlic clove, crushed
2 tablespoons chopped mint
½ teaspoon mustard powder
Rice:
250 g (8 oz) brown rice
600 ml (1 pint) vegetable stock
salt
1 teaspoon ground coriander
2 tablespoons chopped coriander leaves or parsley

Blanch the courgettes and onions or shallots in salted, boiling water for 2 minutes. Drain thoroughly. Trim the courgettes and cut them into 3.5 cm (1½ inch) slices.

Thread all the vegetables and the bay leaves on to 4 wooden skewers and lay them in a shallow dish.

To make the marinade, mix together all the ingredients and pour over the kebabs. Turn in the marinade to coat the vegetables thoroughly. Cover and set aside at room temperature for 2 hours.

To cook the rice, put it in a pan with the stock, salt and ground coriander. Bring to the boil, stir well, cover and simmer for 45 minutes.

Drain the kebabs from the marinade. Place under a preheated moderate grill and cook them for about 8 minutes, turning frequently and brushing with the remaining marinade.

Stir the chopped coriander into the rice and spoon into a heated serving dish. Arrange the kebabs on top and serve at once. Serve with a green salad.

Serves 4

Mixed Vegetable Curry

1 small cauliflower, cut into florets
250 g (8 oz) carrots, sliced
250 g (8 oz) French beans, topped, tailed and sliced
250 g (8 oz) shelled broad beans
175 g (6 oz) frozen sweetcorn
1 large onion, thinly sliced into rings
50 g (2 oz) peanuts
25 g (1 oz) shredded coconut
salt and pepper
Sauce:
25 g (1 oz) soft margarine
25 g (1 oz) wholemeal flour
2 teaspoons curry powder
1 teaspoon ground turmeric
1 teaspoon ground cumin
300 ml (½ pint) milk
2 tablespoons double cream

Steam or boil the cauliflower, carrots, beans, sweetcorn and onion in salted water until they are just tender. Drain and plunge into cold water to prevent further cooking. Drain again.

To make the sauce, melt the margarine and stir in the flour. Cook for 1 minute, then stir in the spices and cook for a further 3 minutes. Gradually stir in the milk, and bring to the boil. Simmer for 3 minutes. Season with salt and pepper and stir in the cream.

Stir the vegetables and peanuts into the sauce and reheat gently.

Turn the mixture into a heated serving dish and sprinkle with the coconut. Serve hot.

Serves 4

right: vegetable kebabs with coriander rice, mixed vegetable curry

Mexican Rice

1 tablespoon sunflower oil

2 onions, sliced

1 red pepper, cored, deseeded
   and chopped

250 g (8 oz) brown rice

600 ml (1 pint) vegetable stock

8 small tomatoes, skinned and
   quartered

1 small avocado, stoned,
   peeled and cut into 1 cm
   (½ inch) chunks

4 eggs

4 tablespoons natural yogurt

salt and pepper

2 tablespoons chopped coriander
   leaves or finely snipped chives,
   to garnish

Heat the oil and fry the onions and
red pepper over a moderate heat for
3 minutes, stirring frequently. Stir
in the rice and cook for 1 minute.
Add the stock and bring to the boil.
Stir once.

Cover the pan, then simmer
gently for 40 minutes.

Add the tomatoes and avocado,
stirring in carefully to avoid
breaking them up. Cover and
simmer for 5 minutes.

Beat the eggs with the yogurt and
season with salt and pepper. Pour
over the rice and fork it over and
over. Cook until the eggs are just
set. Garnish with the chives or
coriander and serve at once.

Serves 4

Millet and Broad Bean Pilaff

250 g (8 oz) millet seeds

600 ml (1 pint) vegetable stock

500 g (1 lb) dried broad beans

2 tablespoons sunflower oil

1 large onion, sliced

250 g (8 oz) courgettes, thinly sliced

1 green pepper, cored, deseeded and
   chopped

2 cardamom pods, seeds removed
   and lightly crushed

1 teaspoon cumin seeds

2 large tomatoes, skinned and sliced

4 tablespoons sultanas

salt and pepper

parsley sprigs, to garnish

Put the millet in a saucepan with
the vegetable stock and add a little
salt. Bring to the boil and stir
thoroughly, then cover the pan and
simmer gently for 20 minutes,
stirring occasionally, until the millet
is tender and all the stock has been
absorbed.

Cook the broad beans in salted,
boiling water according to the
packet instructions until they are
tender. Drain well.

Heat the oil and fry the onion,
courgettes and green pepper over a

left: Mexican rice
right: millet and broad bean pilaff,
vegetable fried rice

moderate heat for 4–5 minutes, stirring frequently. Stir in the crushed cardamom seeds and the cumin seeds, then season with salt and pepper and cook for 1 minute. Add the tomatoes, stir well and simmer for 3 minutes.

Stir the broad beans, sultanas and millet into the vegetables and heat gently. Garnish with the parsley and serve hot.

Serves 4–6

Vegetable Fried Rice

2 large eggs
1 tablespoon water
pepper
15 g (½ oz) butter
2 tablespoons sunflower oil
3 leeks, thinly sliced
250 g (8 oz) button mushrooms, thinly sliced
75 g (3 oz) cashew nuts
125 g (4 oz) frozen peas, defrosted
2 tablespoons soy sauce
250 g (8 oz) cooked brown rice, cold
2 tablespoons chopped mint

Beat the eggs with the water and season with pepper. Melt the butter in an omelette pan and when it is hot, pour in the egg mixture. Tip the pan to spread the mixture evenly and cook over a moderate heat until it is set on 1 side. Flip the omelette over and cook it to brown the other side. Slide it on to a plate and leave to cool.

Heat the oil in a pan and fry the leeks over a moderate heat for 3 minutes, stirring frequently. Add the mushrooms, nuts and peas and stir well. Cook for 1 minute. Stir in the soy sauce and rice and season with pepper. Cook for 5 minutes, stirring frequently.

Cut the omelette into thin strips. Stir the mint into the rice and adjust the seasoning if necessary.

Turn the rice into a heated serving dish and garnish with the omelette strips arranged in a lattice pattern. Serve hot.

Serves 4

Vegetable Moussaka

125 g (4 oz) brown 'continental'
   lentils, soaked overnight and
   drained
500 g (1 lb) tomatoes, skinned
   and chopped
1 bay leaf
1 teaspoon dried oregano
1 teaspoon soft dark brown sugar
2 tablespoons sunflower oil
1 large aubergine, thinly sliced
500 g (1 lb) potatoes, thinly sliced
salt and pepper
Sauce:
25 g (1 oz) soft margarine
25 g (1 oz) wholemeal flour
300 ml (½ pint) milk
150 ml (¼ pint) natural yogurt
125 g (4 oz) feta, crumbled, or
   Wensleydale cheese, grated
1 egg
large pinch of grated nutmeg

Grease a casserole. Cook the lentils in unsalted, boiling water for 40 minutes. Drain.

Simmer the tomatoes with the bay leaf, oregano, sugar, salt and pepper for 20 minutes. Stir in the lentils and simmer for 10 minutes, stirring, until thick.

Heat the oil and fry the aubergine, a few slices at a time, over a moderate heat until they begin to colour.

Cook the potato slices in salted, boiling water for 10 minutes, until they begin to soften. Drain.

Make layers of the tomato and lentil sauce, the aubergines and potatoes in the casserole, finishing with the potatoes.

To make the sauce, melt the margarine and stir in the flour. Cook for 1 minute, then remove the pan from the heat. Gradually stir in the milk, then the yogurt. Bring to the boil, then simmer for 3 minutes. Remove from the heat. Beat in half of the cheese, and the egg and season with salt, pepper and nutmeg. Pour the sauce over the dish and sprinkle the remaining cheese on top.

Stand the casserole on a baking sheet. Place in a preheated oven, 190°C (375°F), Gas Mark 5, and bake for 35–40 minutes until the sauce is bubbling and browned.

Serves 4

Asparagus Quiche

175 g (6 oz) wholemeal
   self-raising flour
50 g (2 oz) white vegetable fat
25 g (1 oz) butter
40 g (1½ oz) cottage cheese, sieved
½–1 teaspoon fennel seeds, lightly
   crushed
cold water, to mix
salt and pepper
Filling:
375 g (12 oz) asparagus spears,
   cooked and drained
75 g (3 oz) low fat soft cheese
150 ml (¼ pint) natural yogurt
6 tablespoons milk
2 eggs

Grease a 20 cm (8 inch) flan ring and stand on a baking tray.

Sift the flour and and a pinch of salt together and tip the bran from the sieve back into the bowl. Rub in the fats until the mixture is like fine breadcrumbs. Stir in the cheese and fennel and mix to a dough with a very little water. Knead the dough lightly. Wrap in clingfilm or foil and chill for at least 30 minutes.

Roll out the pastry on a lightly floured board and use to line the flan ring.

Arrange the asparagus spears in a wheel pattern in the pastry case.

Mix the cheese, yogurt and milk together, beat in the eggs and season with salt and pepper. Pour the filling into the pastry case.

Bake in a preheated oven, 190°C (375°F), Gas Mark 5, for 40–45 minutes until the filling is set. Serve the quiche warm.

Serves 6

*right: vegetable moussaka,
asparagus quiche,
fruity aubergine boats*

Fruity Aubergine Boats

4 aubergines, about 175 g (6 oz)
  each, halved lengthways
5 tablespoons sunflower oil
1 large onion, finely chopped
2 garlic cloves, finely chopped
500 g (1 lb) tomatoes, skinned
  and sliced
75 g (3 oz) sultanas
50 g (2 oz) seedless raisins
75 g (3 oz) blanched, slivered
  almonds
2 tablespoons chopped parsley
½ teaspoon dried thyme

salt and pepper
flat-leaved parsley, to garnish

Grease a baking dish. Scoop out the flesh from the aubergines (a curved grapefruit knife is ideal for this), leaving firm 'walls'. Chop the aubergine flesh finely and put it in a colander. Sprinkle liberally with salt and leave for about 1 hour to degorge (draw off juices).

Rinse the aubergine shells in cold water, then drain and dry them thoroughly on kitchen paper.

Heat the oil and fry the onion, garlic and aubergine over a moderate heat for about 5 minutes, stirring frequently.

Add the tomatoes, stir well and fry for a further 5 minutes.

Stir in the sultanas, raisins, almonds, parsley and thyme and season with salt and pepper.

Stand the aubergine shells, cut side up, in the baking dish and fill them with the tomato mixture.

Place in a preheated oven, 180°F (350°C), Gas Mark 4, and bake the aubergines for 1 hour. Serve hot, garnished with the parsley leaves.

Serves 4

Mushroom Pasta with Pine Nuts

This mushroom sauce has an unexciting appearance but a truly marvellous taste. Be sure to use the flat dark mushrooms; those freshly gathered from the field are best of all. Pine nuts, or pine kernels, are to be found in most health food shops and supermarkets and are an important ingredient in this recipe.

1½ tablespoons vegetable oil
1 medium onion, sliced
625 g (1¼ lb) flat open
   mushrooms, sliced
1–2 teaspoons green peppercorns
1 tablespoon soy sauce
3 tablespoons water
2 tablespoons double or whipping
   cream
375 g (12 oz) pasta shapes (quills,
   spirals or cartwheels)
2 tablespoons pine nuts
salt and pepper
1 tablespoon chopped parsley, to
   garnish

Heat 1 tablespoon of the oil and fry the onion for about 5 minutes. Add the mushrooms and cook for a further few minutes until they have cooked down a little.

Add a pinch of salt, the green peppercorns, soy sauce and water. Cover the pan and simmer gently for about 20 minutes, then remove the lid and cook quickly for about 1 minute to reduce some of the liquid in the pan.

Pour into a blender or food processor and mix very briefly for just a few seconds (the mushrooms should retain some texture). Return to the rinsed pan and stir in the cream. Set aside.

Bring a large pan of salted water to the boil. Add the pasta, stir a couple of times and boil briskly for about 10 minutes until the pasta is just tender. Drain thoroughly.

Meanwhile, heat the remaining oil in a small pan and fry the pine nuts for 30 seconds until golden brown. Drain on kitchen paper and reserve until ready to serve.

To serve, reheat the sauce without boiling and pour over the pasta. Sprinkle with pine nuts and parsley and serve straight away.

Serves 4

Leek and Egg Puffs

1 leek, about 200 g (7 oz), sliced
1 tablespoon vegetable oil
1 small onion, thinly sliced
½ teaspoon coriander seeds,
   crushed
50 g (2 oz) mature Cheddar cheese,
   cut into small cubes
250 g (8 oz) frozen puff pastry,
   thawed
2 hard-boiled eggs, shelled and
   halved lengthways
salt and pepper
beaten egg, for glazing

Cook the sliced leek in boiling salted water for 6 minutes, then drain and set aside.

Heat the oil in a small pan and fry the onion until golden brown. Add salt, pepper and coriander seeds, then stir in the cooked leek.

Allow the mixture to cool slightly and stir in the cheese.

Roll out the pastry thinly and trim to a 30 cm (12 inch) square. Cut it into 4 x 10 cm (4 inch) squares. Cut the trimmings into leaf shapes to garnish the puffs.

Brush the edges of each pastry square with beaten egg. Divide the filling among the squares, placing it just off centre, and top with half a boiled egg. Fold the pastry over to make a triangle.

Seal the edges firmly and brush the tops with beaten egg. Arrange the pastry leaves on top and brush with more beaten egg.

Bake in a preheated oven, 220°C (425°F), Gas Mark 7, for 15–20 minutes until puffed up and golden brown. Serve hot.

Makes 4 puffs

right: mushroom pasta with pine nuts, leek and egg puffs

Vegetable Cobbler

3 carrots, thinly sliced

½ small cauliflower, divided into
   florets

50 g (2 oz) soft margarine

8 small leeks, thickly sliced

2 small heads fennel, sliced

25 g (1 oz) wholemeal flour

150 ml (¼ pint) vegetable stock

2 tablespoons chopped parsley

salt and pepper

fennel fronds, to garnish

Topping:

175 g (6 oz) wholemeal flour

1 teaspoon bicarbonate of soda

75 g (3 oz) oat flakes

40 g (1½ oz) soft margarine

1 large egg

3 tablespoons natural yogurt

50 g (2 oz) Edam cheese, grated

Cook the carrots and cauliflower in boiling salted water for 5 minutes. Drain and place in a casserole.

Melt half the margarine and fry the leeks and fennel over a moderate heat for about 4 minutes, stirring frequently. Transfer to the casserole.

Melt the remaining margarine, stir in the flour and cook for 1 minute. Remove the pan from the heat and gradually stir in the stock. Season with salt and pepper and bring to the boil. Simmer for 3 minutes. Stir in the parsley and pour the sauce over the vegetables. Cover the casserole and place in a preheated oven, 180°C (350°F), Gas Mark 4, for 45 minutes.

To make the topping, sift together the flour, soda and a pinch of salt and tip back the bran from the sieve into the bowl. Add half the oat flakes and mix in the margarine.

Beat in the egg and yogurt to make a firm dough. Shape the dough into a ball and knead until it is smooth.

Roll out the dough on a lightly floured board to 1 cm (½ inch) thick and cut into rounds with a fluted biscuit cutter.

Arrange the rounds on top of the vegetables, then sprinkle with the cheese mixed with the remaining oat flakes. Increase the oven temperature to 200°C (400°F), Gas Mark 6, and bake for 15 minutes until the topping is golden. Garnish with fennel fronds. Serve at once.

Serves 6

above: vegetable cobbler
right: family vegetable pie

34

Family Vegetable Pie

This attractive and tasty pie is topped with a special very light pastry. Remember to put the margarine into the freezer for 1–2 hours before you begin to make the pie.

175 g (6 oz) wholemeal
  self-raising flour
1 teaspoon mixed dried herbs
125 g (4 oz) hard vegetable
  margarine, from the freezer
3 tablespoons water
1 tablespoon vegetable oil
salt and pepper
Filling:
300 ml (½ pint) water
125 g (4 oz) carrots, sliced
125 g (4 oz) leeks, sliced
125 g (4 oz) celery, sliced
125 g (4 oz) cauliflower, cut into
  florets
about 300 ml (½ pint) milk
25 g (1 oz) butter
25 g (1 oz) plain flour
2 tablespoons chopped parsley
250 g (8 oz) can red kidney beans,
  drained
beaten egg, for brushing

Put the flour, ¼ teaspoon salt and the dried herbs into a bowl and grate the margarine into it. Mix lightly with a round-bladed knife to distribute the flakes of margarine, make a well in the centre and add the water and oil.

Mix gently to a firm dough, being careful not to over-handle it. Put the dough into a polythene bag and then chill in the refrigerator while making the filling.

To make the filling, pour the water into a pan, add salt and bring to the boil. Put in the carrots, cover and simmer for 5 minutes, then add the remaining vegetables, cover and cook for 10 minutes.

Strain the vegetables, reserving the liquid. Make this up to a generous 600 ml (1 pint) with milk. Melt the butter in the pan, add the flour and cook gently, stirring, for 3 minutes. Pour in the milk mixture and bring to the boil, stirring all the time, and simmer for 1 minute. Add salt and plenty of pepper, then add the cooked vegetables, parsley and red beans. Pour into a 1.2 litre (2 pint) pie dish with a pie funnel in the centre.

Roll out the pastry into an oval 2.5 cm (1 inch) larger than the pie dish. Cut a strip off to cover the rim of the dish, brush with egg and place the lid in position. Trim and flute the edges. Cut any leftover pastry into decorations for the top of the pie. Brush with beaten egg, arrange the decorations on the pie and brush again with beaten egg.

Bake in a preheated oven, 200°C (400°F), Gas Mark 6, for 25 minutes until the pastry is golden brown.

Serves 4

Two-bean Vegetable Goulash

125 g (4 oz) black beans, soaked
  overnight
125 g (4 oz) cannellini beans, soaked
  overnight
1 tablespoon vegetable oil
125 g (4 oz) very small onions or
  shallots, whole
4 celery sticks, sliced into chunks
4 small courgettes, cut into 2.5 cm
  (1 inch) chunks
3 small carrots, cut lengthways into
  chunks
400 g (13 oz) can tomatoes
300 ml (½ pint) vegetable stock
1 tablespoon paprika
½ teaspoon caraway seeds
1 tablespoon cornflour
2 tablespoons water
salt and pepper
150 ml (¼ pint) soured cream, to
  serve (optional)

Drain the beans and rinse them under cold running water. Put them in 2 separate pans, cover with water and bring to the boil. Boil fast for 10 minutes then lower the heat, half cover the pans and simmer for about 1 hour until tender. Drain, rinse and set aside.

Heat the oil in a large pan with a lid and fry the onions, celery, courgettes and carrots quickly over a high heat until lightly browned.

Pour in the tomatoes with their juice and the stock. Stir in the paprika, caraway seeds, salt and pepper. Cover the pan and simmer for 20 minutes until the vegetables are tender.

Stir both lots of beans into the vegetables. Blend the cornflour with the water and add to the pan.

Bring to the boil, stirring gently until the sauce thickens a little. Cover the pan and simmer again for about 10 minutes.

Spoon the hot goulash into a warm serving dish and serve with soured cream, if liked.

Serves 4

Felafel in Pitta Pockets

2 x 425 g (14 oz) cans chickpeas,
  drained
1 onion, grated
1 garlic clove, crushed (optional)
1 teaspoon ground cumin
1 teaspoon ground coriander
¼ teaspoon ground chilli
½ teaspoon caraway seeds
3 tablespoons chopped parsley
1 egg, beaten
75 g (3 oz) wholemeal flour
vegetable oil, for shallow frying
salt and pepper
To serve:
4 wholemeal pitta breads
½ cucumber, diced
4 small firm tomatoes, quartered
1 bunch watercress
crisp lettuce leaves

Mash the chickpeas to a paste on a large plate, a few at a time, using a fork or potato masher. (This can be done in a food processor if wished). Put them into a bowl with the onion, garlic, cumin, coriander, chilli, caraway seeds, salt and pepper. Mix to a firm paste, then stir in the parsley.

Form the mixture into small balls, then pat them into small flat cakes, about 3.5 cm (1½ inches) across. Dip into beaten egg, then into flour.

Shallow fry in oil in batches for about 5 minutes until crisp and brown. Drain on kitchen paper and keep hot in a preheated oven, 110°C (225°F), Gas Mark ¼, while frying the rest. Warm the pitta bread.

Split the pitta breads along 1 side with a sharp knife and fill the pocket with a mixture of cucumber, tomato, watercress, lettuce leaves and felafels. Serve immediately with Quick Coleslaw (see opposite).

Makes about 20

Popovers with Onion and Tomato Sauce

Onion and Tomato Sauce:

1 tablespoon vegetable oil

1 large onion, thinly sliced

500 g (1 lb) ripe tomatoes,
   skinned and chopped

1 teaspoon soy sauce

2 teaspoons tomato purée

salt and pepper

Batter:

50 g (2 oz) plain wholemeal flour

50 g (2 oz) plain white flour

pinch of cayenne pepper

1 teaspoon mixed dried
   herbs

2 eggs, beaten

1 tablespoon vegetable oil

150 ml (¼ pint) milk

150 ml (¼ pint) water

To make the sauce, heat the oil in a pan and fry the onion for about 10 minutes until brown. Add the tomatoes, soy sauce, tomato purée, salt and plenty of pepper. Bring to simmering point, stirring, then cover the pan and cook gently for 10 minutes.

While the sauce is cooking, make the batter. Put the flours, ½ teaspoon salt, pepper, cayenne and herbs into a bowl. Add the eggs, oil and half the milk and mix to a smooth paste. Gradually whisk in the remaining milk and the water. Pour the batter into a jug.

Generously oil 2 trays of 12 tart tins and put them in a preheated oven, 220°C (425°F), Gas Mark 7, until smoking hot.

Remove from the oven, pour the batter into the tins, almost filling them, and then bake for about 12 minutes until puffed up and golden brown.

Serve the popovers immediately with the hot sauce.

Makes 24

Quick Coleslaw

Make a quick delicious coleslaw by combining ½ small white cabbage, finely shredded, with 2 large carrots, coarsely grated, 1 small onion, grated, salt and pepper and 150 ml (¼ pint) soured cream.

far left: two-bean vegetable goulash
*left: felafel in pitta pockets,
popovers with onion and
tomato sauce*

Provençal Gougère

Choux pastry:

50 g (2 oz) hard vegetable margarine

150 ml (¼ pint) water

65 g (2½ oz) plain wholemeal flour

2 eggs, beaten

½ teaspoon made English mustard

50 g (2 oz) mature Cheddar cheese, grated

salt and pepper

1 tablespoon chopped parsley, to garnish

Filling:

1 tablespoon vegetable oil

1 large onion, coarsely chopped

1 large aubergine, cut into 2.5 cm (1 inch) cubes

3 small courgettes, sliced

1 green pepper, cored, deseeded and diced

1 red pepper, cored, deseeded and diced

300 g (10 oz) tomatoes, skinned, quartered and deseeded

2 tablespoons tomato purée

1 teaspoon sugar

1 tablespoon chopped fresh basil or 1 teaspoon dried basil

Grease a baking sheet. To make the pastry, put the margarine, water and ¼ teaspoon salt in a large pan. Have the flour ready on a small plate nearby. Bring the margarine and water to a fast boil, draw the pan off the heat and tip in the flour all at once.

Beat briskly with a wooden spoon until the mixture forms a ball that rolls cleanly around the pan. Leave to cool for 5 minutes.

Slowly add the beaten eggs, a little at a time, beating well between each addition. (An electric beater makes this job quick and easy.) When all the egg is incorporated,

beat in plenty of pepper, the mustard and the grated Cheddar.

Place adjoining heaped teaspoons of the mixture in a 25 cm (10 inch) circle on the baking sheet, leaving rough peaks.

Bake in a preheated oven, 220°C (425°F), Gas Mark 7, for about 40 minutes until the choux pastry is puffy and brown.

Meanwhile, make the filling. Heat the oil in a pan and fry the onion gently without browning for about 10 minutes. Add the aubergine, courgettes, peppers and tomatoes. Stir in the tomato purée, sugar, basil, salt and pepper.

Cover the pan and simmer gently for a further 15 minutes, stirring once or twice during cooking.

Transfer the hot choux pastry ring to a heated platter and spoon in the filling. Serve immediately, sprinkled with chopped parsley.

Serves 4

Cheesy Pasta with Red Pepper

It is important to use a good strong Cheddar for this homely dish. Leave out the red pepper if you prefer but it supplies contrast in colour, texture and flavour. Remember to reheat the sauce thoroughly after adding the pasta; then all the dish needs is a few minutes under a hot grill.

175 g (6 oz) wholemeal pasta, such as macaroni
salt and pepper
Sauce:
25 g (1 oz) butter
25 g (1 oz) plain white flour
750 ml (1¼ pints) milk
½ teaspoon made English mustard
large pinch of cayenne pepper
¼ teaspoon grated nutmeg
250 g (8 oz) mature Cheddar cheese, grated
1 red pepper, cored, deseeded and cut into 1 cm (½ inch) dice
2 tablespoons chopped fresh parsley (optional)
To garnish:
oil, for shallow frying
3 thin slices wholemeal bread, cut into 12 triangles

Cook the pasta in salted, boiling water for about 15 minutes until just tender. Drain the pasta, rinse and set aside.

To make the sauce, using a pan large enough to accommodate the pasta and sauce, melt the butter, then add the flour and cook for 3 minutes, stirring. Pour in the milk and bring to the boil, stirring all the time until the sauce thickens. Simmer for 3 minutes.

Add salt and pepper, the mustard, cayenne and nutmeg, then stir in all but 25 g (1 oz) of the grated Cheddar. Blanch the red pepper pieces in boiling water for 2 minutes, then stir into the cheese sauce. Now add the cooked pasta and reheat thoroughly but gently. Stir in the chopped parsley if using.

Either divide the mixture among 4 individual ovenproof dishes or put it into 1 large shallow ovenproof dish. Sprinkle with the remaining cheese and place under a preheated medium grill for about 4 minutes to brown the top.

Meanwhile, make the garnish. Heat the oil in a frying pan to a depth of 1 cm (½ inch) and fry the triangles of bread for a few seconds on both sides until golden brown. Drain on kitchen paper.

Remove the cheesy pasta from underneath the hot grill and arrange some fried bread triangles around the edge of the dish(es).

Serves 4

Crunchy Egg Tacos

6 taco shells

2 tomatoes, sliced, to garnish

Filling One:

7 eggs

3 tablespoons milk

15 g (½ oz) butter

2 tablespoons chopped capers

2 tablespoons chopped parsley

salt and pepper

Filling Two:

1 tablespoon olive oil

300 g (10 oz) bean sprouts

1–2 tablespoons soy sauce

Warm the taco shells in a preheated oven, 110°C (225°F), Gas Mark ¼, while preparing the fillings. Try to cook both fillings at the same time; they only take a few minutes.

To make Filling One, whisk the eggs, milk, salt and pepper together in a bowl. Melt the butter in a small pan and stir the eggs over a low heat to scramble them slightly. When almost ready, stir in the capers and parsley.

To make Filling Two, heat the olive oil until smoking in a frying pan, add the bean sprouts and, keeping the heat high, stir-fry for about 2

minutes, adding the soy sauce, some salt and plenty of black pepper.

Take the taco shells from the oven, spoon the bean sprout filling into the bottom, then top with the scrambled egg filling.

Garnish with slices of tomato and serve immediately.

Serves 2–3

Spiced Brown Rice with Broccoli

Although bright green broccoli looks attractive, several other vegetables could be used for this recipe: courgettes, mushrooms or peppers, for instance. Pine nuts, which have a lovely creamy taste, are readily available in supermarkets and health food shops. Thawed frozen broccoli can also be used instead of fresh.

right: crunchy egg tacos, spiced brown rice with broccoli
far right: *courgette and watercress flan*

15 g (½ oz) butter

1 onion, finely sliced

175 g (6 oz) long-grain brown rice

450 ml (¾ pint) vegetable stock

175 g (6 oz) broccoli, cut into thin
   strips lengthways

1 tablespoon olive oil

50 g (2 oz) pine nuts

½ teaspoon garam masala
   (optional)

salt and pepper

Melt the butter and fry the onion until golden. Add the rice and fry gently for 2–3 minutes. Pour in the stock and bring to the boil, then cover the pan, lower the heat and simmer gently for 35–40 minutes until the rice is cooked but still slightly chewy, and all the stock has been absorbed.

About 15 minutes before the rice is cooked, cook the broccoli. Heat the olive oil in a large frying pan and stir-fry the broccoli for about 10 minutes. If you like the broccoli soft rather than slightly crisp, cover the pan for part of the time. This will create steam, which will soften the broccoli further.

When the broccoli is cooked to taste add the pine nuts to the pan and stir-fry until they are lightly browned. Stir in the cooked rice, adding pepper and a little salt if necessary (the stock may have provided enough salt).

Spoon into a serving dish, sprinkle lightly with garam masala, if liked, and serve immediately,

Serves 2

Courgette and Watercress Flan

A delicately flavoured flan which is perfect hot with brown rice but equally good cold, with a tomato salad.

Pastry:

175 g (6 oz) plain wholemeal flour

¼ teaspoon salt

75 g (3 oz) hard vegetable margarine

3 tablespoons water

1 tablespoon vegetable oil

Filling:

1 tablespoon vegetable oil

3 small courgettes, about
   125 g (4 oz), sliced

2 bunches watercress, stalks removed

2 eggs

150 ml (¼ pint) soured cream

5 tablespoons milk

pinch of gated nutmeg

pepper

To make the pastry, put the flour and salt in a bowl and rub in the margarine until the mixture resembles fine breadcrumbs. Using a round-bladed knife, mix to a firm dough with the water and oil. The oil will help to keep the pastry moist and light.

Roll out on a floured surface and use to line a 20 cm (8 inch) fluted flan ring. Place on a baking sheet and bake in a preheated oven, 200°C (400°F), Gas Mark 6, for 15 minutes to set the pastry without browning.

Meanwhile, make the filling. Heat the oil in a pan and fry the courgettes quickly on both sides until brown. Drain on kitchen paper. Fry the watercress for 30 seconds until soft, then chop coarsely. Distribute the courgettes and watercress evenly in the flan.

Put the eggs, soured cream, milk, salt, pepper and nutmeg into a bowl and whisk together.

Pull the centre shelf of the oven out slightly and place the flan case on it, then pour the egg and cream mixture over the courgettes and slide the shelf gently into place. This avoids spilling the liquid on the way to the oven.

Bake for 25 minutes until the flan is set and lightly browned.

Serves 4

Vegetable Stir-fried Rice

1½ tablespoons olive oil

125 g (4 oz) carrots, cut into matchstick strips

125 g (4 oz) small button mushrooms, thinly sliced

1 small green pepper, cored, deseeded and thinly sliced

3 spring onions, finely sliced

50 g (2 oz) frozen peas

4 eggs, beaten

300 g (10 oz) long-grain brown rice, cooked and dried

2 tablespoons soy sauce

salt and pepper

4 spring onion frills, to garnish (see page 62)

Heat ½ tablespoon of the oil in a wok or large frying pan and stir-fry the carrots, mushrooms, pepper, spring onions and peas for about 3 minutes until lightly cooked but still crisp. Remove from the wok.

Heat another ½ tablespoon of oil in the wok, pour in the eggs and stir-fry until cooked and lightly set. Remove and keep warm.

Add the remaining oil and stir-fry the rice for 2 minutes. Add the soy sauce, a little salt and a generous amount of black pepper.

Return the vegetables and egg to the wok, stirring gently over a low heat. Serve piping hot, garnished with the spring onion frills.

Serves 3–4

Frittata

25 g (1 oz) butter

4 eggs, beaten

300 g (10 oz) spinach, cooked and lightly chopped, or 125 g (4 oz) frozen spinach, cooked

3 firm tomatoes, skinned and coarsely chopped

125 g (4 oz) cooked potatoes, diced, or 75 g (3 oz) cooked brown rice

1 teaspoon chopped sage

few drops of Tabasco sauce

salt and pepper

Heat half the butter in a large frying pan until sizzling. Pour in the beaten eggs and stir for a few seconds over a moderate heat.

Allow the eggs to settle in the pan and then distribute the spinach, tomatoes and potatoes or rice evenly over the surface.

Sprinkle with salt, pepper, sage and Tabasco sauce. Cook gently for about 4 minutes until the underside is set and golden brown. Gently lift the edge with a fish slice to check.

When the underside is done, tip the omelette out upside-down on to a large plate, add the remaining butter to the pan, run it round over the heat to coat the base, then slide the omelette back into the pan and cook the other side for about 3 minutes. Cut into quarters and serve hot or cold.

Serves 2

Indian Lentil Cakes

250 g (8 oz) green or brown lentils, washed, soaked overnight and drained

450 ml (¾ pint) vegetable stock

1 tablespoon oil

1 onion, finely sliced

1 green pepper, cored, deseeded and finely chopped

1 teaspoon ground cumin

1 teaspoon ground coriander

1 teaspoon chilli powder

1 egg, beaten

125 g (4 oz) jumbo or porridge oats

salt and pepper

oil, for frying

Put the lentils and stock in a pan. Bring to the boil and simmer gently for 40 minutes until all the stock is absorbed and the lentils are tender.

Heat the oil and fry the onion for 10 minutes without browning. Add the pepper, cook for 4 minutes, then stir in the spices, lentils, salt and pepper. Mix and cool, then shape into round flat cakes.

Dip into egg, then into oats to coat completely. Shallow fry for 6 minutes, turning once, until brown and crisp. Drain on kitchen paper.

Makes 8–10

right: vegetable stir-fried rice, frittata, Indian lentil cakes

Coriander Chickpea Casserole

375 g (12 oz) dried chickpeas, soaked
  overnight and drained
1 small onion, quartered
a few parsley sprigs
2 tablespoons sunflower oil
1 large onion, sliced
2 garlic cloves, finely chopped
4 celery sticks, thinly sliced
2 carrots, thinly sliced
1 red pepper, cored, deseeded and
  thinly sliced
2 teaspoons ground coriander
375 g (12 oz) tomatoes, skinned and
  sliced
150 ml (¼ pint) vegetable stock
2 tablespoons chopped coriander
  leaves, or parsley
salt and pepper

Put the chickpeas in a pan with the quartered onion and parsley, cover with water and bring to the boil. Cover and fast-boil for 5 minutes. Reduce the heat and simmer for 2 hours until the chickpeas are tender. Drain the chickpeas.

Heat the oil in a flameproof casserole and fry the sliced onion, garlic, celery, carrots and red pepper over a moderate heat for 4 minutes, stirring frequently. Stir in the ground coriander and then cook gently for 1 minute.

Add the tomatoes, stock, drained chickpeas, half the chopped herbs and season with salt and pepper. Bring to the boil and stir well.

Cover, place in a preheated oven, 120°C (250°F), Gas Mark ½, and cook for 2 hours. Taste and adjust the seasoning if necessary. Garnish with the remaining chopped herbs.

Serves 4

Stuffed Mediterranean Vegetables

2 aubergines, halved lengthways
2 large courgettes, haved lengthways
2 large beefsteak tomatoes
  or 4 small ones, halved
4 large flat field mushrooms
  or 8 smaller ones
about 1 tablespoon vegetable oil, for
  brushing
about 6 tablespoons water
salt and pepper
Stuffing:
1 tablespoon vegetable oil
1 garlic clove, crushed (optional)
1 large onion, chopped
125 g (4 oz) mushrooms, chopped
200 g (7 oz) fresh wholemeal
  breadcrumbs
2 teaspoons dried basil or
  2 tablespoons chopped fresh basil
½ teaspoon yeast extract
¼ teaspoon cayenne pepper
To garnish:
2 teaspoons vegetable oil
2 tablespoons pumpkin seeds
1 tablespoon chopped parsley

Hollow out the centres of the aubergines and cut the flesh into small pieces. Prepare the courgettes in the same way. Sprinkle the aubergine and courgette pieces with salt and leave for 1 hour. The salt will draw out the bitter juices.

Blanch the aubergine and courgette shells in boiling water for

2 minutes, then drain and set aside.

Scoop out the tomato flesh and seeds into a bowl. Trim the stalks of the mushrooms, chop and reserve.

Brush all the vegetable cases with oil, inside and out, and arrange in 2 roasting pans.

To make the stuffing, heat the oil in a pan and fry the garlic and onion for about 10 minutes until golden brown. Add the mushroom stalks, chopped mushrooms, breadcrumbs, basil, yeast extract, salt, pepper and cayenne.

Dry the aubergine and courgette pieces and add them to the pan with the flesh from the tomatoes.

Mix the stuffing, then spoon it into the prepared vegetable cases.

Pour 2–3 tablespoons of water into each roasting pan, then place in a preheated oven, 200°C (400°F), Gas Mark 6, and bake for about 20 minutes until just tender.

Make the garnish. Heat the oil in a small pan and fry the pumpkin seeds for 1–2 minutes until browned. Drain on kitchen paper, cool and mix with the parsley, then sprinkle over the stuffed vegetables.

Serves 4

Spiced Beans and Pasta

1 tablespoon vegetable oil
3 onions, chopped
2 garlic cloves, crushed
3 tablespoons curry powder
½ teaspoon ground cumin
½ teaspoon ground coriander
½ teaspoon ground chilli
2 teaspoon grated fresh root ginger
2 tablespoons wholemeal flour
900 ml (1½ pints) vegetable stock
1 tablespoon lemon juice
150 g (5 oz) pasta shapes
2 x 425 g (14 oz) cans red kidney
  beans, drained, liquor reserved
salt

Heat the oil in a pan and gently fry the onions and garlic for 5 minutes. Stir in the spices and flour. Cook for 1 minute. Pour in the stock and lemon juice, bring to the boil, cover and simmer gently for 25 minutes. Taste and add salt if necessary.

Meanwhile, prepare the pasta. Cook in plenty of boiling salted water for about 10 minutes, or according to packet instructions, until tender. Drain and rinse.

Add the pasta and beans to the sauce. Thin with the reserved bean liquor if necessary. Serve piping hot with a selection of accompaniments.

Serves 4

far left: coriander chickpea casserole
left: stuffed Mediterranean vegetables, spiced beans and pasta

Roulade with Wine and Mushroom Filling

Filling:

2 teaspoons vegetable oil

1 shallot or small onion, finely chopped

250 g (8 oz) button mushrooms, chopped

150 ml (¼ pint) dry white wine and vegetable stock mixed or 150 ml (¼ pint) vegetable stock

3 tablespoons double or whipping cream

salt and pepper

1 bunch watercress, chopped, plus a few sprigs, to garnish

Roulade:

5 eggs, separated

½ teaspoon made English mustard

1 teaspoon vinegar

125 g (4 oz) grated mature Cheddar cheese

1 tablespoon grated Parmesan cheese

Line a 23 x 33 cm (9 x 13 inch) Swiss roll tin with nonstick baking paper or greased greaseproof paper.

Make the filling by heating the oil in a pan with a lid and frying the shallot or onion for 5 minutes until tender but not brown. Add the mushrooms and cook for 2–3 minutes. Pour in the wine and stock and add a little salt and pepper.

Cover the pan and cook for about 5 minutes, then remove the lid and boil rapidly to reduce the liquid to about 2 tablespoons. Stir in the cream and set aside.

To make the roulade, whisk the egg yolks, salt, pepper, mustard and vinegar in a small bowl until light and thick. Fold in the grated Cheddar cheese.

In a large bowl whisk the egg whites until stiff. Take 2 tablespoons of the whisked whites and fold them into the cheese and yolk mixture to loosen it, then spoon it into the remaining whites and gently fold together until the mixtures are evenly blended.

Pour into the prepared tin and gently smooth the surface. Bake near the top of a preheated oven, 200°C (400°F), Gas Mark 6, for 10–12 minutes until risen and golden brown. Remove from the oven. Leave the oven on.

Sprinkle a sheet of greaseproof paper with Parmesan cheese and turn the roulade on to it. Peel off the baking paper.

Gently reheat the mushroom filling mixture, but do not allow it to boil, and spoon it evenly over the roulade. Sprinkle the filling mixture with watercress, then roll the roulade up tightly, just like a Swiss roll.

Lift carefully on to a warm serving dish and replace in the oven for about 4 minutes to heat the roulade through.

Serve the roulade piping hot, garnished with watercress sprigs.

Serves 4

Crumbly Nut Roast

40 g (1½ oz) butter

1 onion, chopped

1 celery stick, chopped

250 g (8 oz) mixed nuts (walnuts, brazils and hazelnuts in equal quantities), coarsely chopped

3 large tomatoes, about 250 g (8 oz), skinned and chopped

175 g (6 oz) fresh wholemeal breadcrumbs

1 teaspoon mixed dried herbs

¼ teaspoon ground chilli

2 eggs, lightly beaten

salt and pepper

watercress sprigs, to garnish

Rich Brown Gravy (right), to serve

Oil a 500 g (1 lb) loaf tin and line the base with oiled greaseproof paper or nonstick baking paper.

Melt the butter in a large pan and fry the onion and celery gently for 5 minutes without browning.

Add the nuts, tomatoes, breadcrumbs, salt, pepper, mixed herbs, chilli and eggs and mix to a fairly soft consistency. Taste and adjust the seasoning if necessary.

Spoon into the prepared tin, cover with oiled baking foil and bake in a preheated oven, 220°C (425°F), Gas Mark 7, for 50–60 minutes, until the nut roast is firm.

Ease off the foil and run a knife around the sides of the tin. Turn out on to a warm dish, garnish with watercress and serve with gravy.

Serves 4

Rich Brown Gravy

15 g (½ oz) butter

15 g (½ oz) plain flour

450 ml (¾ pint) hot water

1 teaspoon yeast extract

1 teaspoon tomato purée

1 tablespoon soy sauce

pepper

Melt the butter in a small pan, add the flour and stir for 3 minutes over a fairly high heat until the flour turns golden brown.

Remove from the heat and pour in the water. Add the yeast extract, tomato purée, soy sauce and pepper

Bring to the boil, still stirring, and simmer for 3–5 minutes until the gravy has reduced to a nice rich brown. Pour the gravy into a warmed jug and serve hot.

Makes 450 ml (¾ pint)

Side Dishes

Okra and Mushrooms with Sunflower Seeds

2 teaspoons vegetable oil
2 tablespoons sunflower seeds
375 g (12 oz) okra, topped and tailed
25 g (1 oz) butter
125 g (4 oz) white button
   mushrooms, halved
salt and pepper

Heat the oil in a small pan and cook the sunflower seeds for 1–2 minutes until brown. Drain them on kitchen paper and set aside.

It is best to cook the okra whole, but if any are too large cut them in half lengthways.

Melt the butter in a frying pan or wok and stir-fry the okra quickly for 3–4 minutes. Add the mushrooms and cook for a further 3–4 minutes.

Sprinkle with salt and pepper, cover the pan and leave to cook for about 10 minutes, by which time the mushrooms should be soft and the okra crisply tender.

Remove the lid and cook quickly for 1–2 minutes to reduce the liquid in the pan.

Spoon into a warm dish and sprinkle with the sunflower seeds.

Serves 4

New Potatoes with Fennel and Mint

1 kg (2 lb) tiny new potatoes
15 g (½ oz) butter
1 small fennel bulb, trimmed and
   finely chopped
salt and pepper
2 tablespoons chopped mint, plus
   mint sprigs, to garnish

Bring a pan of salted water to the boil, and add the potatoes. Simmer for about 15 minutes until tender, then drain.

Put the butter into the warm pan and heat gently. Add the fennel and fry for about 5 minutes until just beginning to brown, then season well with pepper.

Tip the cooked potatoes into the pan, add the mint and toss the potatoes so that they are coated with butter, mint and fennel.

Serve the potatoes hot, garnished with mint sprigs.

Serves 4

Summer Vegetables with Yogurt and Mint

250 g (8 oz) shelled broad beans
salt
250 g (8 oz) runner beans, strings
   removed and sliced
250 g (8 oz) shelled peas
150 ml (¼ pint) natural yogurt
1 tablespoon chopped mint
salt and black pepper

Cook the broad beans for 8 minutes in a little boiling salted water, then drain well.

Cook the runner beans and peas together for 5 minutes and drain. Season with black pepper.

Heat the yogurt gently in one of the vegetable pans. Serve the vegetables, drizzled with the warm yogurt and garnished with the chopped mint.

Serves 4

right: okra and mushrooms with sunflower seeds,
new potatoes with fennel and mint,
summer vegetables with yogurt and mint

Celeriac Sticks with Mustard

750 g (1½ lb) celeriac, thickly sliced
  and cut into 1 x 7 cm (½ x 3 inch)
  chips
1 tablespoon lemon juice
salt and pepper
Dressing:
150 ml (¼ pint) double or whipping
  cream or natural yogurt
1 tablespoon wholegrain mustard
To garnish:
lemon slices
coriander leaves or parsley sprigs

Put the celeriac chips in a pan with
a pinch of salt and the lemon juice
and cover with water. Bring to the
boil, cover and simmer for 15–20
minutes until the celeriac is
tender but still firm. Drain and
keep warm.

Pour the cream or yogurt into
the rinsed pan and stir in the salt,
pepper and mustard. Heat very
gently until hot, but do not boil.

Pour the cream and mustard
dressing over the celeriac and
garnish with lemon slices and the
coriander leaves or parsley sprigs.

Serves 4

Lemon Cabbage with Poppy Seeds

The contrast provided by the green
and white cabbages gives a
particularly attractive appearance
to this simple vegetable dish.
It can be served with almost any
main meal.

150 ml (¼ pint) water
375 g (12 oz) hard white
  cabbage, shredded

375 g (12 oz) spring greens or green cabbage, shredded

25 g (1 oz) butter, cut into small pieces

grated rind of 1 lemon

1½ teaspoons poppy seeds

salt and pepper

2–3 tablespoons soured cream, to serve (optional)

Put the water into a large pan, add ½ teaspoon salt and bring to the boil. Add the white and green cabbages, cover and simmer steadily for 7–10 minutes. The cabbage should be crisply tender and most of the water absorbed.

Take the lid off the pan and boil quickly until any remaining liquid is reduced.

Add the pieces of butter, lemon rind, poppy seeds and lots of pepper. Stir briefly until the butter is melted and the cabbage well coated.

Spoon the hot cabbage into a warm serving dish and serve with some soured cream spooned over the top, if liked.

Serves 4

left: celeriac sticks with mustard, lemon cabbage with poppy seeds
***right:** bean and bean sprout stir-fry*

Bean and Bean Sprout Stir-fry

An interesting and quickly prepared vegetable side dish. If fresh beans are used, blanch them for 1 minute in boiling water, then drain well and pat dry before stir-frying.

15 g (½ oz) butter

1 tablespoon olive oil

300 g (10 oz) French beans, blanched for 1 minute in boiling water, or frozen whole green beans

300 g (10 oz) bean sprouts

2 teaspoons paprika

salt and pepper

Heat the butter and oil in a wok or large frying pan until foamy, then add the beans and stir-fry gently for about 4 minutes.

Push them to the sides of the wok, turn the heat up a little and add the bean sprouts. Stir-fry for about 2 minutes.

Now mix the beans and bean sprouts together, adding a little salt, plenty of pepper and the paprika. Stir-fry for 1 minute more, then turn into a warm serving dish and serve. Alternatively, serve straight from the wok.

Serves 4

Cauliflower with Peanut Sauce

1 cauliflower, about 500 g (1 lb), cut
   into florets
salt and pepper
2 tablespoons chopped salted
   peanuts, to garnish
Sauce:
15 g (½ oz) butter
15 g (½ oz) plain flour
150 ml (¼ pint) milk
150 ml (¼ pint) vegetable stock
4 tablespoons crunchy peanut butter
½ teaspoon yeast extract

Cook the cauliflower in boiling
salted water for about 6–8 minutes;
it should still be slightly crisp. Drain
and keep warm in a serving dish.

Meanwhile, make the sauce. Melt
the butter in a small pan, add the
flour and cook for 3 minutes,
stirring all the time.

Pour in the milk and vegetable
stock and bring to the boil, still
stirring. Simmer for 2–3 minutes,
then stir in the peanut butter, a
spoonful at a time. The peanut
butter will thicken the sauce.

Add the yeast extract, a little salt,
if necessary, and some pepper.

Pour the peanut sauce over the
cauliflower and sprinkle with the
chopped peanuts. Serve hot.

Serves 4

Kartoshki

15 g (½ oz) butter
1 tablespoon oil
500 g (1 lb) small potatoes, unpeeled
   and fairly thickly sliced
salt and black pepper
2 spring onions, chopped, to garnish

Heat the butter and oil in a large
frying pan until it is sizzling.

Add the potatoes and stir until
evenly coated and glistening. Fry
them quickly over a high heat until
golden brown but not cooked.

Turn the slices and sprinkle
generously with salt and pepper.
Cover the pan, lower the heat and
continue to cook for about 20
minutes until the slices are tender,
shaking the pan occasionally to
prevent them sticking.

Remove the lid and turn up the
heat again for 1–2 minutes. Serve
sprinkled with spring onions.

Serves 2–3

Braised Onions in Cider

2 large Spanish onions, about 500 g (1 lb)
1 tablespoon vegetable oil
300 ml (½ pint) dry cider
2 teaspoons chopped fresh sage
1 teaspoon cornflour
1 tablespoon water
salt and pepper

Remove the papery skins from the
onions and cut each into 4. Trim
the bases very lightly so that the
quarters stay intact during cooking.

Heat the oil in a frying pan and
quickly fry the onion quarters on all
sides until golden brown. Place
them in a small shallow casserole,
cut-side up.

Pour the cider into the pan with
the salt, pepper and sage. Bring to
the boil, then pour over the onions.

Cover the casserole and bake in a
preheated oven, 180°C (350°F), Gas
Mark 4, for 40 minutes.

Remove from the oven, blend the
cornflour with the water and stir
into the liquid surrounding the
onions. Cover again and replace in
the oven for a further 20 minutes by
which time the onions will be
tender and the sauce will be slightly
thickened. Serve hot.

Serves 4

right: cauliflower with peanut sauce,
kartoshki,
braised onions in cider

Spinach Vinaigrette

750 g (1½ lb) young spinach
40 g (1½ oz) pine nuts, or blanched
   slivered almonds
1 small onion, thinly sliced into rings
   (optional), to garnish
lemon slices, to serve
Dressing:
4 tablespoons olive oil
1 tablespoon lemon juice
2 tablespoons chopped mint
½ teaspoon soft light brown sugar
salt and pepper

Wash the spinach and cook in the water clinging to the leaves in a large pan for 5 minutes or until tender. Drain in a colander, gently pressing out the water without damaging any of the leaves.

To make the dressing, mix all the ingredients together.

Mix the spinach in the dressing and stir in the pine nuts. Serve just warm or cool — but not chilled. Garnish with onion rings, if liked, and serve with lemon slices.

Serves 4

Potato and Parsnip Layer

500 g (1 lb) potatoes, cut into 5 mm
   (¼ inch) slices
1 large onion, thinly sliced into rings
250 g (8 oz) parsnips, cut into 5 mm
   (¼ inch) slices
25 g (1 oz) soft margarine
pinch of grated nutmeg
300 ml (½ pint) milk or buttermilk
salt and pepper

Grease a baking dish well. Make layers of potato, onion and parsnip in the dish. Dot the potatoes with margarine and season each layer with salt, pepper and nutmeg, finishing with potatoes. Pour over the milk or buttermilk.

Stand the dish on a baking sheet and cover with a lid or foil. Place in a preheated oven, 180°C (350°F), Gas Mark 4, and bake for 2 hours. Remove the covering for the last 30 minutes to brown the potatoes. Serve hot.

Serves 4

Artichoke Nests

750 g (1½ lb) Jerusalem artichokes
1 tablespoon lemon juice
150 ml (¼ pint) vegetable stock
25 g (1 oz) soft margarine
4 tablespoons milk
pinch of grated nutmeg
1 tablespoon chopped mint
1 egg
25 g (1 oz) ground almonds
salt and pepper

Grease a baking sheet. Cook the artichokes in the lemon juice and stock for 15 minutes or until tender.

Drain and mash them with the margarine, milk, salt, pepper, nutmeg and mint. Beat in the egg and almonds, beating well to make a smooth thick paste. Cool slightly. Using a piping bag fitted with a large round nozzle, pipe the artichoke paste on to the baking sheet to make 4 round 'nests'.

Bake in a preheated oven, 180°C (350°F), Gas Mark 4, for 20 minutes until firm. Fill the nests with cooked vegetables of your choice.

Serves 4

*right: spinach vinaigrette,
potato and parsnip layer,
artichoke nests*

Broad Beans with Sesame

500 g (1 lb) shelled broad beans,
  fresh or frozen
2 tablespoons sesame seeds
25 g (1 oz) butter
1 tablespoon lemon juice
salt and pepper

Cook the beans in boiling salted water until tender, 8–15 minutes depending on whether they are fresh or frozen.

Toast the sesame seeds under a preheated moderate grill until they are evenly browned.

Drain the beans and put the butter in the pan. Melt it quickly and, when just beginning to brown, add the lemon juice and pepper.

Tip the beans back into the pan and toss well in the butter. Serve sprinkled with the sesame seeds.

Serves 4

Corn on the Cob with Herbs

4 corn cobs, husks and threads
  removed
50 g (2 oz) butter
2 teaspoons chopped mixed
  fresh herbs (parsley, thyme
  and chives)
salt and pepper

Boil the corn cobs in unsalted water for 15 minutes and drain well.

Blend the butter, seasoning and herbs. Spread a little over each corn cob and wrap each one in baking foil, crimping the edges together.

Place on a baking sheet and bake in a preheated oven, 200°F (400°C), Gas Mark 6, for 20 minutes. Unwrap the corn and pour over the juices.

Serves 4

Colcannon

250 g (8 oz) shredded white cabbage
500 g (1 lb) potatoes, cooked and
  mashed without milk or butter
25 g (1 oz) butter
1 onion, chopped
2 teaspoons poppy seeds
salt and pepper

Cook the cabbage in a little boiling salted water for about 6 minutes until crisply tender. Drain and put into a bowl with the mashed potato.

Melt half the butter in a pan and fry the onion until golden. Stir into the cabbage and potato, adding a little salt and lots of pepper.

Use the remaining butter to grease a 500 g (1 lb) loaf tin, and coat it inside with the poppy seeds.

Spoon in the cabbage mixture, smooth the top and cover with foil. Bake in a preheated oven, 200°C (400°F), Gas Mark 6, for 40 minutes.

Serves 4

Parsnips with Breadcrumbs

500 g (1 lb) very small parsnips
1 tablespoon vegetable oil
75 g (3 oz) fresh wholemeal
  breadcrumbs
2 tablespoons freshly grated
  Parmesan cheese
salt and pepper
1 tablespoon chopped parsley, to
  garnish

Lightly oil an ovenproof dish. Cook the parsnips in boiling salted water for 7–10 minutes until just tender. Drain and return to the pan.

Toss them in the oil and plenty of pepper. Mix the breadcrumbs, Parmesan cheese and ½ teaspoon salt, add to the pan and toss again.

Spoon the parsnips into the ovenproof dish and bake near the top of a preheated oven, 220°C (425°F), Gas Mark 7, for 15–20 minutes until the top is crisp and lightly browned.

Garnish with chopped parsley and serve immediately.

Serves 4

*right: broad beans with sesame,
corn on the cob with herbs,
colcannon,
parsnips with breadcrumbs*

Leek, Potato and Coriander Bake

Use a waxy type of potato, such as a Cyprus or Jersey, for this dish. Cook in a large shallow roasting pan so that the potatoes and leeks are spread in a single layer and become nicely browned. Serve as a main course or as an accompaniment to almost any dish.

1 tablespoon oil
25 g (1 oz) butter
500 g (1 lb) leeks, cut into 1.5 cm (¾ inch) slices
1 kg (2 lb) small potatoes, unpeeled and cut into 1 cm (½ inch) cubes
1 teaspoon black peppercorns
2 teaspoons coriander seeds
1 teaspoon sea salt

Put the oil and butter into a large shallow roasting pan and place in a preheated oven, 200°C (400°F), Gas Mark 6, until the butter is melted.

Add the leeks and potatoes, turning them over several times to coat them with the oil and butter.

Crush the peppercorns with the coriander seeds. If you have no pestle and mortar, put the seeds and peppercorns between double sheets of kitchen paper or greaseproof paper, then crush them firmly with a rolling pin.

Put the crushed peppercorns and coriander seeds in a small bowl. Add the salt, then sprinkle evenly over the potatoes and leeks and stir them through.

Cover the pan tightly with foil, then bake in the oven for 45 minutes. After this time, remove the foil, turn the potatoes and leeks over and put back near the top of the oven for a further 30 minutes to become brown. Serve hot.

Serves 4

Pan-braised Peppers with Tomato

A vegetable recipe full of flavour and colour. It is not essential to use different coloured peppers, but it does look attractive. This dish is wonderful hot and almost as good served cold with a salad selection.

1 tablespoon vegetable oil

2 onions, roughly chopped

3 large peppers, red, green and
 yellow, total weight about
 500 g (1 lb), cored, deseeded and
 cut into strips

500 g (1 lb) tomatoes, skinned and
 chopped

1 teaspoon coriander seeds

1 teaspoon black peppercorns

½ teaspoon salt

½ teaspoon ground chilli

Heat the oil in a large frying pan and fry the onions for about 5 minutes until golden.

Add the peppers and cook gently for 2–3 minutes, then stir in the chopped tomatoes.

Crush the coriander seeds and peppercorns. Use a pestle and mortar if you have one; otherwise put the seeds and peppercorns between double sheets of kitchen paper or greaseproof paper and crush them with a rolling pin.

Add the salt and chilli to the crushed seeds and peppercorns and sprinkle the mixture over the peppers and tomatoes. Mix together lightly, cover the pan and cook gently for 20 minutes.

Serves 4

left: *leek, potato and coriander bake,* *pan-braised peppers with tomato,* *button mushrooms with green* *peppercorns*

Button Mushrooms with Green Peppercorns

A simple but unusual way to serve button mushrooms which also makes a delicious starter. Green peppercorns are sold either in jars or small cans in most delicatessens or large stores. They are quite soft and so can be crushed easily.

1 tablespoon olive oil

500 g (1 lb) small white button
 mushrooms

4 tablespoons water

4 slices brown bread,
 crusts removed

2 tablespoons vegetable oil

25 g (1 oz) butter

3 teaspoons green peppercorns,
 lightly crushed

2 tablespoons double or
 whipping cream

salt

coriander leaves or parsley
 sprigs, to garnish

Heat the olive oil in a large frying pan and fry the mushrooms quickly for about 5 minutes until just beginning to brown.

Add the water and a little salt, cover the pan and simmer for about 10 minutes, by which time there will be a fair amount of liquid in the pan.

Meanwhile, cut the bread into 1 cm (½ inch) dice. Heat the oil and butter in a frying pan until sizzling and add the diced bread. Fry quickly until golden brown, then drain on kitchen paper.

Gently heat the peppercorns and cream. Tip the mushrooms into a warm serving dish and scatter with the bread croûtons. Pour the warm cream and peppercorn sauce over the mushrooms.

Garnish with coriander leaves or parsley sprigs and serve at once.

Serves 4

Salads

Grapefruit Salad

The salad is a tangy accompaniment to grilled poultry, meat and fish, and makes an interesting starter.

3 grapefruit, pink if available, peeled and segmented
10–12 heads corn salad or 1 bunch watercress
½ small Cos lettuce, torn into small pieces
75 g (3 oz) halved almonds, blanched and toasted
Dressing:
3 tablespoons olive oil
2 shallots, finely chopped
1 tablespoon lemon juice
1 teaspoon clear honey
salt and pepper

Toss together the grapefruit and corn salad or watercress. To make the dressing, mix the ingredients until well blended, pour over the salad and toss well.

Line a serving dish with the lettuce leaves. Just before serving, stir the toasted almonds into the grapefruit salad and spoon it carefully on to the bed of lettuce.

Serves 4–6

Fruit and Nut Salad

250 g (8 oz) shelled broad beans
1 apple, cored and thinly sliced
2 pears, peeled, cored and sliced
1 tablespoon water
1 tablespoon lemon juice
1 orange, peeled and segmented
1 bunch watercress
2 tablespoons macadamia nuts
2 tablespoons walnut halves
Dressing:
150 ml (¼ pint) natural yogurt
2 tablespoons orange juice
1 tablespoon clear honey
2 tablespoons chopped mint
1 spring onion, thinly sliced
salt and pepper

To make the dressing, mix all the ingredients in a small bowl.

Cook the broad beans in boiling salted water until just tender. Drain, cool in cold water, then drain again.

Toss the apple and pears in the water and lemon juice, then drain.

Mix together the beans, apple, pears, orange segments, watercress and nuts. Toss with the dressing and serve.

Serves 4–6

Domino Salad

1 small cauliflower, divided into florets
125 g (4 oz) dried chickpeas, soaked overnight and cooked
4 tablespoons black olives
1 bunch watercress
chicory leaves, to serve
Dressing:
3 tablespoons olive oil
1 tablespoon cider vinegar
1 hard-boiled egg, roughly chopped
1 tablespoon soured cream
salt and pepper

Cook the cauliflower in boiling salted water for about 8 minutes until it is barely tender. Drain, plunge into cold water and drain again. Leave to cool.

Mix the dressing in a blender to emulsify the ingredients. Taste and adjust the seasoning if necessary.

Mix the cauliflower, chickpeas, olives and watercress. Pour on the dressing and toss well together.

Line a dish with the chicory leaves and arrange the salad on top.

Serves 4

right: grapefruit salad, domino salad, fruit and nut salad

Sprouted Bean Salad

This salad can be served as a first course or as a crunchy side dish.

4 spring onions, green leaves partly
　trimmed
250 g (8 oz) sprouted beans or
peas, such as alfalfa or mung beans
4 spring onions, thinly sliced
½ small cucumber, diced
8 large radishes, thinly sliced
4 tablespoons cashew nuts
2 hard-boiled eggs, quartered

salt and pepper
Dressing:
150 ml (¼ pint) natural yogurt
1 teaspoon clear honey
2 teaspoons soy sauce
1 teaspoon red wine vinegar
1 tablespoon dry sherry

To make spring onion frills, remove the roots from the spring onions and trim to about 7 cm (3 inches). Make 6 cuts lengthways through each stalk to within 3.5 cm (1½ inches) of the end. Soak in iced water for about 30 minutes.

To make the dressing, mix the ingredients together until well blended and then pour into 4 individual serving bowls.

Toss together the sprouted beans, spring onions, cucumber, radish slices and cashew nuts. Divide the salad among the bowls and toss again so the salad is well coated with the dressing.

Arrange the egg wedges on top of the salad. Garnish each dish with a spring onion frill.

Serves 4

Piquant Potato Salad

If you cannot find really small potatoes, then use slightly larger ones and cut them in half after cooking. This potato salad can be served as part of a salad selection or it makes a perfect accompaniment to the Courgette and Watercress Flan (see page 41).

750 g (1½ lb) tiny new potatoes
Dressing:
3 tablespoons olive oil
1 tablespoon white wine vinegar
½ teaspoon made English mustard
2 teaspoons capers, finely chopped
1 pickled gherkin, finely chopped
1 tablespoon chopped parsley
salt and pepper

Wash the potatoes and place in a pan of boiling salted water. Cook for 15–20 minutes until just tender. Drain and tip into a bowl.

While the potatoes are cooking make the dressing. Put the oil and vinegar into a small bowl and stir in the salt, pepper, mustard, capers and gherkin. Add the parsley.

Pour the dressing over the hot potatoes and stir gently to coat them all thoroughly. Leave to cool but do not chill.

Serve the potato salad in a shallow dish at room temperature.

Serves 4

Spinach and Mushroom Salad

250 g (8 oz) fresh young spinach leaves, stems removed
125 g (4 oz) small button mushrooms, thinly sliced
1 quantity Light French Dressing (see page 67)
1 head chicory, separated into leaves

Wash the spinach leaves in several changes of water. Pat dry on kitchen paper and snip the leaves into narrow strips, 1 cm (½ inch) wide.

Mix the mushrooms into the spinach. Pour the dressing over and toss the salad until well coated.

Place in a serving bowl, tuck in some leaves of chicory and serve.

Serves 4

Quick and Crunchy Salad

This vitamin-rich salad should always be prepared just before serving so that it is crisp and fresh. It looks attractive when served on a bed of lettuce.

375 g (12 oz) carrots, coarsely grated
3 Cox's Orange Pippins, cored and sliced
1 tablespoon lemon juice
1 tablespoon sunflower seeds
3 tablespoons raisins
2 teaspoons vegetable oil
2 tablespoons cashew nuts
1 quantity Light French Dressing (see page 67)
lettuce leaves, to serve

Put the grated carrot into a large bowl. Sprinkle the apple slices with lemon juice to prevent them discolouring, then add to the bowl.

Lightly mix in the sunflower seeds and raisins.

Heat the oil in a small pan and lightly brown the cashew nuts. Lift out and drain on kitchen paper, then add to the bowl.

Spoon the French dressing over the salad and toss lightly. Serve on a bed of lettuce leaves.

Serves 4

left: sprouted bean salad
above: quick and crunchy salad

Mixed Salad Choice

This colourful selection of salads takes time to assemble, but the result is well worth the effort. It makes the perfect self-service lunch or evening snack.

175 g (6 oz) grated carrot

25 g (1 oz) raisins

125 g (4 oz) can sweetcorn, drained

50 g (2 oz) small button mushrooms, sliced

175 g (6 oz) bean sprouts

1 small green pepper, cored, deseeded and finely sliced

175 g (6 oz) iceberg lettuce, shredded

125 g (4 oz) cucumber, unpeeled and diced

4 celery sticks, chopped

2 red apples, cored and diced

1 tablespoon lemon juice

6 small firm tomatoes, sliced

2 spring onions, sliced

6 hard-boiled eggs, shelled and quartered (optional)

paprika, to sprinkle (optional)

250 g (8 oz) cottage cheese

50 g (2 oz) seedless grapes, halved

To serve:

Piquant Creamy Dressing (see page 65)

Lemon and Mustard Dressing (see page 65)

Hot Garlic Bread (see page 65)

Prepare the various combinations of salads as indicated above and either arrange them separately on a single large platter or on 6 individual small serving dishes.

Make the two dressings and then prepare the garlic bread.

Lay out the buffet and allow guests to choose their own combinations of different salads and dressings. Serve with the warm garlic bread

Serves 6

Piquant Creamy Dressing

150 ml (¼ pint) mayonnaise
150 ml (¼ pint) soured cream
12 stuffed olives, finely chopped
2 teaspoons grated onion
2 teaspoons tomato purée
pinch of chilli powder
2 tablespoons chopped parsley
salt and pepper

Mix the mayonnaise and soured cream together in a bowl, then stir in the olives, onion, tomato purée, salt, pepper and chilli powder.

Adjust the seasoning to taste, then sprinkle with parsley.

Makes 300 ml (½ pint)

Lemon and Mustard Dressing

175 ml (6 fl oz) olive oil
2 tablespoons lemon juice
grated rind of 1 lemon
1 teaspoon caster sugar
1 teaspoon salt and pepper
½ teaspoon English mustard powder

Whisk all the ingredients together in a bowl until well combined.

Makes 175 ml (6 fl oz)

Hot Garlic Bread

150 g (5 oz) butter
¼ teaspoon salt
3 garlic cloves, crushed
2 wholemeal French loaves, cut into
   5 cm (2 inch) slices

Using a fork, blend together the butter, salt and garlic.

Spread the garlic butter on both sides of each slice of bread and put the slices back together to reshape the loaves. Wrap in foil and bake in a preheated oven, 220°C (425°F), Gas Mark 7, for 10 minutes. Unwrap and serve immediately.

Serves 4

Chillied Red and Yellow Salad

This is an easy salad to serve for a winter lunch with some granary bread and unsalted butter. Spinach Soup (see page 8) would make a good starter.

400 g (13 oz) can red kidney
   beans, drained
200 g (7 oz) can sweetcorn,
   drained
4 celery sticks, chopped
1 Spanish onion, very thinly
   sliced into rings
mustard and cress,
   to garnish
chicory leaves, to serve

Dressing:
6 tablespoons olive oil
1 tablespoon wine vinegar
½ teaspoon Tabasco sauce
½ teaspoon mustard powder
2 green chillies, deseeded and finely
   chopped, or to taste
salt and pepper

Put the beans, sweetcorn, celery and onion into a bowl.

To make the dressing, mix all the ingredients together well. Pour over the bean mixture and turn lightly to coat thoroughly with the dressing.

Spoon into a serving dish and leave covered for 1–2 hours to allow the flavours to mature.

Just before serving, garnish with the mustard and cress and add the chicory leaves.

Serves 4

Note: Can marinate for up to 8 hours, covered in clingfilm in the refrigerator.

left: mixed salad choice, spinach and mushroom salad (see page 63)
above: chillied red and yellow salad

Tropical Salad

An unusual and delicious salad. You will find coconut flakes or slices in many health food shops but unsweetened desiccated coconut can be used instead. You can use a 425 g (14 oz) can of pineapple if fresh fruit is not available.

300 g (10 oz) brown long-grain rice, cooked
50 g (2 oz) dried coconut flakes
½ cucumber, unpeeled and cut into 1 cm (½ inch) cubes
1 small ripe pineapple, peeled, cored and cut into 2.5 cm (1 inch) pieces
1 tablespoon olive oil
1 teaspoon lemon juice
salt and pepper
To garnish:
2 teaspoons olive oil
50 g (2 oz) whole blanched almonds
pineapple leaves

Put the rice, coconut, cucumber and pineapple pieces into a bowl.

Add the oil and lemon juice and a little salt and pepper. Taste and adjust the seasoning if necessary, then spoon into a serving dish.

To garnish, heat the oil in a small pan, add the almonds and then fry quickly until golden brown.

Scatter the almonds over the salad and add the pineapple leaves.

Serves 4

Fennel Salad

2 fennel bulbs, thinly sliced
1 small lettuce heart, shredded
2 oranges, peeled and thinly sliced into rings
1 bunch watercress, divided into sprigs
50 g (2 oz) currants
50 g (2 oz) walnut halves
Dressing:
3 tablespoons sunflower oil
1 tablespoon orange juice
1 teaspoon grated orange rind
1 teaspoon red wine vinegar
1 tablespoon sunflower seeds, crushed
salt and pepper

Mix the dressing ingredients in a bowl until well blended.

Toss the sliced fennel and the shredded lettuce together.

Make a ring of the orange slices around the outside of a serving dish. Arrange the watercress sprigs in a ring inside them.

Just before serving, toss the fennel and lettuce in the dressing and pile the salad in the centre of the dish. Make a ring of currants around the green salad and scatter with nuts.

Serves 4–6

Orange and Bean Salad

Nutritionally this crisp colourful salad has everything. It is good in the winter too, when other salad ingredients are sometimes expensive.

4 large oranges
400 g (13 oz) can red kidney beans, drained
300 g (10 oz) bean sprouts
4 celery sticks, thinly sliced
watercress sprigs, to garnish

Light French Dressing:
5 tablespoons olive oil
2 tablespoons lemon juice
¼ teaspoon sugar
¼ teaspoon made English mustard
salt and pepper

Using a serrated knife, cut off the top and bottom from each orange, then remove all the skin and pith, leaving a ball of fruit. Cut into segments by cutting down on either side of each membrane, and put in a bowl with any juice that runs out while cutting.

Add the beans, bean sprouts and celery and toss lightly together.

To make the dressing, put the oil, lemon juice, sugar, salt, pepper and mustard into a screw-top jar and shake vigorously until blended. Just before serving the salad, spoon over the dressing and garnish with the watercress sprigs.

Serves 4

left: fennel salad
below: tropical salad, orange and bean salad

Desserts

Winter Rhubarb Jelly

Use tender forced rhubarb when available; summer garden rhubarb can be used, but will not supply the same delicate colour.

500 g (1 lb) pink forced rhubarb, cut into 2.5 cm (1 inch) lengths
2 tablespoons soft light brown sugar
4 tablespoons water
¼ teaspoon ground cinnamon
150 ml (¼ pint) fresh orange juice
4 tablespoons clear honey
1 teaspoon agar agar
8 honey oat biscuits, crumbled (optional)

Put the rhubarb in a pan with the sugar, water and cinnamon. Cover and cook gently for about 10 minutes until the rhubarb has softened to a pulp.

Meanwhile, put the orange juice, honey and agar agar into a small pan and bring to the boil.

Pour on to the rhubarb and stir well. Taste for sweetness and add extra honey if necessary.

Pour the mixture into a large glass dish, cover and chill overnight.

Just before serving, sprinkle with crumbled biscuits, if liked.

Serves 4

Cranachan with Fruit Kissel

Kissel:
500 g (1 lb) fresh or frozen soft fruits (choose 3–4 from raspberries, redcurrants, loganberries, strawberries, blackcurrants or blackberries)
50 g (2 oz) light soft brown sugar
150 ml (¼ pint) unsweetened orange juice
2 teaspoons cornflour
2 tablespoons water
Cranachan:
150 ml (¼ pint) double or whipping cream
150 ml (¼ pint) single cream
few drops vanilla essence
1 tablespoon soft light brown sugar
40 g (1½ oz) coarse oatmeal, toasted

To make the kissel, put the fruits into a bowl. Frozen fruits need not be thawed.

Dissolve the sugar in the orange juice over a low heat. Mix the cornflour to a smooth paste with the water and add to the pan. Bring to the boil, stirring, until the sauce clears and thickens.

Pour over the fruit and stir gently. Cover and chill in the refrigerator for at least 3 hours.

To make the cranachan, whip the 2 creams together until they form soft peaks, add the vanilla, then fold in the sugar and all but 2 teaspoons of the toasted oatmeal.

Spoon the cranachan into a dish and sprinkle with the reserved oatmeal. Serve with the kissel.

Serves 4

Melon and Raspberries in Sauternes

1 small ripe Galia melon
175 g (6 oz) fresh raspberries
½ bottle Sauternes, chilled

Halve the melon and scoop out small balls using a melon baller.

Divide the melon and raspberries equally among 4 glass dishes. Pour over any melon juice, cover and chill for at least 2 hours.

Just before serving, pour the chilled Sauternes into each dish to almost cover the fruit.

Serves 4

right: winter rhubarb jelly, cranachan with fruit kissel, melon and raspberries in Sauternes

Brandy Junket with Green Fruit Salad

This junket, a sophisticated version of the gentle childhood pudding, should be set in small dishes, and the fruit salad should be served in 1 large dish so that they are served separately but enjoyed together. The junket may be made without brandy if preferred. Feijoa fruit can be found in some greengrocers and large supermarkets.

Brandy Junket:

450 ml (¾ pint) milk

150 ml (¼ pint) single cream

1 tablespoon soft light brown sugar

2 tablespoons brandy

1 teaspoon vegetarian junket rennet

freshly grated nutmeg

Green Fruit Salad:

50 g (2 oz) caster sugar

150 ml (¼ pint) water

1 tablespoon lemon juice

75 g (3 oz) seedless green grapes, halved

2 kiwi fruit, sliced

2 feijoa fruit, sliced (or lychees, pitted)

½ Galia melon, cut into 1 cm (½ inch) cubes

2 crisp green apples, quartered, cored and sliced

mint sprigs, to decorate

To make the junket, pour the milk and cream into a pan and warm until just tepid. Stir in the sugar until dissolved, then add the brandy and rennet.

Pour the junket into 4 small dishes, grate a little nutmeg on top of each dish and leave to stand at room temperature for about 1 hour to set, then chill for at least 3 hours.

To make the fruit salad, put the sugar, water and lemon juice into a small pan, bring to the boil and simmer for 1 minute. Leave the syrup until cold.

Arrange the fruits in a dish and pour over the cold syrup. Cover and chill until ready to serve with the chilled junkets.

Decorate the fruit salad with mint before serving.

Serves 4

Note: Both the junket and fruit salad can be prepared up to 8 hours in advance, then covered and kept chilled in the refrigerator.

Strawberry and Yogurt Ice

This fruity ice cream has a strong fruity taste and a light texture.

125 g (4 oz) caster sugar

300 ml (½ pint) water

375 g (12 oz) fresh strawberries

300 ml (½ pint) strawberry yogurt

1 egg white

150 ml (¼ pint) double or whipping cream

Put the sugar and water into a small pan and heat gently to dissolve the sugar, then boil rapidly until the thread stage is reached (see note). Leave to cool.

Reserve 4 strawberries for decoration, slice the rest and put into a blender or food processor with the syrup. Blend for a few seconds and pour into a bowl.

Stir in the yogurt and pour into a 1.2 litre (2 pint) freezer container. Freeze for about 2 hours, stirring once or twice, until mushy.

Spoon the strawberry mixture into a large mixing bowl and put the egg white and cream into slightly smaller bowls.

Whisk the egg white until stiff but not dry. Whisk the cream until it forms soft peaks, and beat the strawberry mixture until smooth. There is no need to wash the whisk in between if you keep to this order.

With a large metal spoon, turn the egg white and cream into the strawberry mixture and gently fold all the mixtures together until smoothly blended.

Pour into the container and freeze for about 3 hours until the ice cream is setting round the edges. Spoon into a bowl and whisk again until smooth and light (this prevents hard crystals forming in the ice cream).

Pour back into the container, cover and freeze for at least 6 hours.

Take the ice cream from the freezer about 40 minutes before serving and transfer to the refrigerator to soften slightly. Scoop

or spoon the ice cream into glasses and serve decorated with the reserved strawberries.

Serves 4

Note: When boiling sugar syrup, the thread stage temperature is 110°C (225°F) on a sugar thermometer. To test without a sugar thermometer, just remove a little of the syrup with a small spoon and allow it to fall from the spoon on to a cold dish. The syrup should form a fine thread.

above: brandy junket with green fruit salad, strawberry and yogurt ice, cider pears with passion fruit

Cider Pears with Passion Fruit

A simple recipe using fresh pears with the tropical taste of passion fruit.

4 large ripe pears, peeled, halved and cored
pared strips of rind from 1 lemon
300 ml (½ pint) dry cider
2 tablespoons clear honey
4 ripe passion fruit, halved

Put the pear halves into a large pan, cut-side up. Add the strips of lemon rind, then pour over the cider and honey. Bring slowly to the boil, cover the pan and lower the heat. Simmer gently for about 10 minutes until the pears are tender.

Lift the pears from the syrup with a slotted spoon and arrange them in a shallow serving dish.

Remove the lemon rind from the syrup, turn the heat up and boil quickly for about 5 minutes to reduce it a little. Leave it to cool for a few minutes.

Scoop the passion fruit seeds and flesh into the syrup, stir briefly, then spoon over the pears. Cover, then chill in the refrigerator for about 3 hours before serving.

Serves 4

Pears Brûlée

This delicious combination of two classic recipes is perfect for a dinner party. It is best served in individual portions but can also be made in one large shallow ovenproof dish.

4 ripe pears, peeled, quartered and cored
300 ml (½ pint) red wine
200 g (7 oz) soft light brown sugar
2 teaspoons arrowroot or cornflour
2 tablespoons water
300ml (½ pint) double or whipping cream
150 ml (¼ pint) natural yogurt, beaten

Halve each pear quarter. Place the pears in a large pan with the wine and 75 g (3 oz) of the sugar and bring slowly to the boil, making sure that the sugar has dissolved. Simmer, covered, for 10 minutes until the pears are just tender.

Remove the pears with a slotted spoon and arrange in 4 small ovenproof dishes.

Turn up the heat and boil the wine syrup quickly to reduce to about 150 ml (¼ pint). Blend the arrowroot with the water and stir into the syrup. Boil for 1 minute until the syrup clears and thickens.

Spoon some syrup over the pears, cover and chill for 1 hour.

Whip the cream until it forms soft peaks, but take care not to overwhip. Fold in the yogurt.

Spoon the cream and yogurt on to the 4 dishes, covering the pears completely. Cover and chill in the refrigerator for at least 4 hours.

Sprinkle the remaining sugar evenly all over the cream and place the dishes under a preheated grill for about 2 minutes until the sugar is caramelized. Serve immediately.

Serves 4

Apricot and Orange Sorbet

Serve this fruity ice on its own or with fresh oranges that have been steeped in apricot liqueur (see note).

150 g (5 oz) caster sugar
300 ml (½ pint) water
75 ml (3 fl oz) orange juice
3 tablespoons lemon juice
grated rind of 1 orange
625 g (1¼ lb) ripe apricots, halved and pitted
1 egg white
orange slices, to decorate (optional)

Put the sugar, water, orange and lemon juices and orange rind into a pan and bring to the boil, stirring until the sugar has dissolved.

Increase the heat and boil rapidly for about 5 minutes until the thread stage is reached (see page 71).

Add the apricots and simmer gently for 2 minutes until they have softened slightly. Leave them to cool in the syrup.

Pour the fruit and syrup into a liquidizer or food processor and blend until smooth. Pour into a freezer container, cover and freeze for about 2 hours until frozen round the sides but mushy in the centre.

Tip into a bowl and whisk briefly until smooth. Whisk the egg white until it forms soft peaks and fold into the fruit using a metal spoon.

Pour back into the container and freeze for about 6 hours.

About 1 hour before serving, take the sorbet from the freezer and put in the refrigerator to soften slightly.

Arrange scoops of sorbet in 4 individual glasses and decorate with orange slices.

Serves 4

Note: Using a serrated knife, cut the top and bottom off 4 oranges, place each one flat on a plate and cut away the skin and pith. Cut into segments by cutting down on either side of each membrane and place the segments in a bowl with any juice from the plate. Stir in 4–6 tablespoons of apricot liqueur (or orange liqueur, if preferred), cover and chill in the refrigerator for 3–4 hours.

left: pears brûlée,
apricot and orange sorbet
right: *blackberry and almond flan*

Blackberry and Almond Flan

Pastry:
75 g (3 oz) plain wholemeal flour
75 g (3 oz) plain white flour
75 g (3 oz) hard vegetable margarine
3 tablespoons water
1 tablespoon vegetable oil
salt
Filling:
175 g (6 oz) blackberries
25 g (1 oz) soft light brown sugar
2 teaspoons lemon juice
2 teaspoons cornflour
2 tablespoons water
Topping:
50 g (2 oz) soft vegetable margarine
50 g (2 oz) soft light brown sugar
1 egg, beaten
65 g (2½ oz) fresh wholemeal
  breadcrumbs
25 g (1 oz) ground almonds
a few drops almond essence
Decoration:
25 g (1 oz) flaked almonds
1 tablespoon caster sugar

To make the pastry, put the flours and salt into a bowl and rub in the margarine until the mixture resembles fine breadcrumbs.

Using a round-bladed knife, mix to a firm dough with the water and oil. The oil helps to keep wholemeal pastry moist and light.

Roll out the pastry on a lightly floured surface and line a 20 cm (8 inch) fluted flan ring. Place on a baking sheet and then bake in a

preheated oven, 200°F (400°C), Gas Mark 6, for 15 minutes to set the pastry. Remove from the oven and lower the heat to 180°C (350°F), Gas Mark 4.

Meanwhile, make the filling. Put the blackberries, sugar and lemon juice in a pan and cook for about 5 minutes until the juice runs.

Blend the cornflour and water and stir into the fruit. Bring to the boil and stir gently until it thickens and clears. Leave to cool.

To make the topping, cream the margarine and sugar until fluffy. Beat in the egg, then fold in the breadcrumbs, ground almonds and almond essence. Spoon the filling into the flan case. Arrange small spoonfuls of topping over the fruit, spreading it out a little. There is no need to cover the fruit completely.

Sprinkle the flaked almonds on top, then bake for 25–30 minutes until firm and lightly browned.

Dredge with caster sugar while still hot and serve.

Serves 4

Hot Spiced Peaches

4 large ripe fresh peaches
grated rind of 1 lemon
¼ teaspoon ground cinnamon
2 tablespoons clear honey
15 g (½ oz) butter

To skin the peaches, dip them into boiling water and the skins will slide off easily. Cut each peach in half and twist to separate the halves, then remove the stone.

Arrange the peach halves cut-side up in an ovenproof dish. Sprinkle with the lemon rind and cinnamon, then spoon over the honey.

Place a dot of butter in the cavity of each peach, cover the dish and bake in a preheated oven, 180°C (350°F), Gas Mark 4, for about 20 minutes until the peaches are tender and juicy. Serve hot with cream or ice cream.

Serves 4

Plum Cheesecake

Quark is a soft cheese made with skimmed milk and so is very low in fat. It is available in health food shops and most large supermarkets, but the cheesecake is equally good made with curd cheese if preferred. The cheesecake

will rise in the oven and drop slowly as it cools, cracking slightly. Do not worry; this is just as it should be.

Base:
125 g (4 oz) self-raising flour
25 g (1 oz) light soft brown sugar
50 g (2 oz) hard vegetable margarine
2 tablespoons vegetable oil
Filling:
500 g (1 lb) ripe red plums, halved
  and pitted
¼ teaspoon ground cinnamon
250 g (8 oz) quark or curd cheese
100 g (3½ oz) light soft brown sugar
2 teaspoons vanilla essence
150 ml (¼ pint) soured cream
1 tablespoon plain white flour
3 eggs, separated
icing sugar, for dusting

Grease a 20 cm (8 inch) loose-bottomed cake tin.

To make the base, put the flour, sugar, margarine and oil into a bowl and knead together to form a soft dough. Press the dough evenly over the base of the cake tin.

Bake near the top of a preheated oven, 180°C (350°F), Gas Mark 4, for 20 minutes until golden brown. Remove and leave to cool in the tin. Reduce the oven heat to 160°C (325°F), Gas Mark 3.

To make the filling, arrange the plum halves close together over the base in the tin, cut-side down. Sprinkle with the cinnamon.

Put the quark or curd cheese, 50 g (2 oz) of the sugar, vanilla essence, soured cream, flour and egg yolks into a bowl and whisk together.

In another bowl, whisk the egg whites until stiff, then whisk in the remaining 50 g (2 oz) sugar. Fold lightly into the cheese mixture and spoon into the tin, over the plums.

Bake in the centre of the oven for 1¼ hours until the top is brown and firm to the touch, then turn off the oven and slightly open the door. Leave the cheesecake to cool in the open oven for 1 hour.

Run a knife round the edge of the cheesecake to loosen it and gently ease it out of the tin.

Slide the cheesecake on to a plate and chill for up to 3 hours before serving, if time allows.

Dust very lightly with icing sugar before serving.

Serves 6–8

Fig and Honey Custard Tart

Pastry:
75 g (3 oz) plain wholemeal flour
75 g (3 oz) plain white flour
75 g (3 oz) hard vegetable margarine
1 egg yolk
1 tablespoon water
1 tablespoon vegetable oil
pinch of salt

right: hot spiced peaches,
plum cheesecake,
fig and honey custard tart

Filling:

175 g (6 oz) dried ready-to-eat figs, sliced

3 tablespoons clear honey

1 tablespoon lemon juice

150 ml (¼ pint) single cream

4 tablespoons milk

1 egg, beaten

1 tablespoon coarsely chopped walnuts

To make the pastry, put the flours and salt into a bowl and rub in the margarine until the mixture resembles fine breadcrumbs. Make a well in the centre, add the egg yolk, water and oil. Mix to a dough, using a round-bladed knife.

Roll out the pastry on a floured surface and line a 20 cm (8 inch) fluted flan ring. Place on a baking sheet and bake in a preheated oven, 200°C (400°F), Gas Mark 6, for 15 minutes to set the pastry without browning. Remove and cool in the tin on a wire rack. Reduce the oven heat to 190°C (375°F), Gas Mark 5.

Meanwhile, make the filling. Put the figs into a small bowl with the honey and lemon juice, stir well, cover and leave to soak for about 1 hour to absorb most of the liquid.

Spoon the figs into the flan and arrange evenly over the base of the cooked pastry case.

Stir the cream and milk into the beaten egg. Pour over the figs and sprinkle the walnuts on top.

Bake for about 20 minutes until the custard is just set and not browned. Cool the tart in the tin on a wire rack. Serve warm or cold.

Serves 4

Pear Clafouti

40 g (1½ oz) wholemeal flour

40 g (1½ oz) soft light brown sugar

2 eggs

1 egg yolk

1 tablespoon sunflower oil

300 ml (½ pint) milk

500 g (1 lb) dessert pears, such as
    Conference, peeled, cored and
    sliced

1 tablespoon lemon juice

2 tablespoons demerara sugar

salt

Grease a shallow baking dish. Mix together the flour, a pinch of salt and the sugar. Beat in the eggs, the egg yolk and the oil. Gradually add the milk, beating constantly until smooth.

Toss the pears in the lemon juice and arrange them in the baking dish. Pour on the batter.

Bake the pudding in a preheated oven, 180°C (350°F), Gas Mark 4, for 30 minutes. Dust with the demerara sugar and bake for a further 10–15 minutes. Serve hot.

Serves 4

Plum Soufflés

500 g (1 lb) dessert plums, stoned

2 teaspoons lemon juice

2 tablespoons water

2 tablespoons wholemeal semolina

2 tablespoons ground almonds

2 eggs, separated

2 tablespoons Amaretto liqueur
    (optional)

4 tablespoons blanched flaked
    almonds, toasted

Grease 4 individual soufflé dishes. Simmer the plums with the lemon juice and water until they are tender. Press them through a sieve. Return the purée to the pan and stir in the semolina. Bring to the boil and simmer for 10 minutes. Cool.

Beat the ground almonds into the cooled purée. Beat in the egg yolks and liqueur, if used.

Whisk the egg whites until they are stiff. Fold them gently into the fruit mixture.

Spoon the plum mixture into the soufflé dishes. Stand them in a roasting pan with water to come halfway up the sides.

Bake the soufflés in a preheated oven, 190°C (375°F), Gas Mark 5, for 20 minutes or until the mixture is just set.

Scatter the almonds on top and serve at once.

Serves 4

Gingered Fruits

500 g (1 lb) mixed dried fruits —
    apple rings, apricots, peaches,
    pears, prunes, soaked overnight in
    600 ml (1 pint) water

1 piece fresh root ginger, peeled and
    halved

4 tablespoons ginger wine

2 teaspoons lemon juice

2 apples, cored and thinly sliced

2 tablespoons blanched almonds,
    toasted

Sauce:

250 ml (8 fl oz) natural yogurt

2 pieces preserved ginger, finely
    chopped

1 tablespoon ginger syrup

1 teaspoon lemon juice

Put the fruits in a pan with the remaining soaking water, the pieces of ginger, ginger wine and lemon juice and bring slowly to the boil. Simmer for 25 minutes until the fruits are tender. Leave to cool.

Remove the ginger. Stir in the apple slices and, just before serving, the toasted almonds.

Mix together the yogurt, chopped ginger, syrup and lemon juice.

Serve the fruits cold but not chilled, with the sauce separately.

Serves 6

*right: pear clafouti,
gingered fruits,
plum soufflés*

Blackcurrant Sesame Crumble

Plain yogurt or soured cream go well with this pudding.

375 g (12 oz) blackcurrants, stripped from stalks

250 g (8 oz) cooking apples, peeled, cored and thinly sliced

2 tablespoons water

40 g (1½ oz) soft light brown sugar

Topping:

150 g (5 oz) wholemeal flour

75 g (3 oz) hard margarine

25 g (1 oz) toasted sesame seeds

40 g (1½ oz) demerara sugar

1 teaspoon ground cinnamon

Simmer the blackcurrants and apples with the water for 5 minutes. Stir in the sugar. Turn the mixture into a shallow baking dish.

To make the topping, rub together the flour and margarine until the mixture resembles fine breadcrumbs, then stir in the sesame seeds, sugar and cinnamon. Sprinkle the topping over the fruit.

Stand the dish on a baking sheet. Bake in a preheated oven, 160°C (325°F), Gas Mark 3, for 40–45 minutes until the topping is golden brown. Serve hot or warm.

Serves 4–6

above: greengage brandy snap cups, apple sorbet, blackcurrant sesame crumble

Apple Sorbet

150 ml (¼ pint) dry white wine
50 g (2 oz) soft light brown sugar
strip of thinly pared lemon rind
2 tablespoons lemon juice
piece of fresh root ginger, peeled
500 g (1 lb) cooking apples, peeled,
    cored and sliced
small angelica or other herb leaves, to
    decorate

Put the wine, sugar, lemon rind,
lemon juice and ginger into a pan
and stir over a low heat until the
sugar has dissolved. Increase the
heat and bring to the boil.

Add the apple slices and poach
them for 8–10 minutes until they
are tender. Remove from the heat
and leave to cool.

Discard the lemon rind and
ginger and purée the fruit and juice
in a blender or press through a
sieve. Pour into a container, cover
with foil and freeze for 1 hour.

Turn the mixture into a chilled
bowl and beat it to break down the
ice crystals. Return to the freezer for
3–4 hours until firm.

To serve, transfer the sorbet to the
refrigerator for about 30 minutes to
soften. Serve it in scoops, decorated
with the herb leaves.

Serves 4

Greengage Brandy Snap Cups

50 g (2 oz) wholemeal flour
½ teaspoon ground ginger
50 g (2 oz) soft light brown sugar
2 tablespoons clear honey
50 g (2 oz) soft margarine
½ teaspoon lemon rind
1 teaspoon lemon juice
1 orange, for making the cups
scented geranium leaves, to decorate
Filling:
500 g (1 lb) greengages, stoned
2 tablespoons water
3 tablespoons clear honey
300 ml (½ pint) natural yogurt

Mix together the flour and ginger.
Heat the sugar, honey and margarine over a low heat and stir
together until the ingredients are
well blended. Remove the pan
from the heat, tip in the flour
and beat well. Beat in the lemon
rind and lemon juice.

Line a baking sheet with nonstick baking paper. Drop tea-
spoonfuls of the mixture on to
the baking sheet, leaving plenty
of space between them. Bake in a
preheated oven, 190°C (375°F),
Gas Mark 5, for 8–10 minutes.

Remove the brandy snaps, 1 at
a time, and, working very quickly
before they harden, press each
brandy snap over an orange held
in the palm of your hand to form

the cups. Place the brandy snap
cups upside-down on a wire rack
to cool. When they are completely cold, they can be stored in an
airtight tin.

To make the filling, reserve
3 greengages to decorate and simmer the remainder in the water
and honey. When the greengages
are soft, press them through a
sieve. Return the purée to the pan
and simmer until thick. Cool.

Beat together the cooled purée
and the yogurt.

Just before serving, fill the cups
with the purée. Cut the reserved
greengages into thin slices and
arrange a few on each cup to
form a flower shape. Place some
scented geranium leaves in the
centre of each 'flower'.

Serves 6

Christmas Pudding

250 g (8 oz) soft margarine

2 eggs, beaten

125 g (4 oz) wholemeal flour

125 g (4 oz) fresh breadcrumbs

1 teaspoon mixed ground spice

1 teaspoon ground cinnamon

½ teaspoon ground nutmeg

250 g (8 oz) seedless raisins

250 g (8 oz) currants

125 g (4 oz) sultanas

250 g (8 oz) dried stoned dates, chopped

50 g (2 oz) dried figs, chopped

50 g (2 oz) blanched chopped almonds

50 g (2 oz) hazelnuts, chopped

3 tablespoons molasses

2 tablespoons orange rind

4 tablespoons orange juice

150 ml (¼ pint) milk

4 tablespoons brandy

Grease 2 x 900 ml (1½ pint) pudding basins. Beat the margarine and gradually beat in the eggs. In a separate bowl, mix together the flour, breadcrumbs and spices and stir into the egg mixture with all the remaining ingredients. Beat until the liquid has been incorporated.

Divide between the pudding basins. Cover with greased greaseproof paper and foil, pleated along the centre to allow for rising.

Place the basins on a trivet in 2 pans and pour in fast-boiling water to come halfway up the sides. Cover the pans and steam for 4 hours, topping up with more boiling water as needed.

Lift out the puddings and cool them on a wire rack. Replace the covers with some fresh greased greaseproof paper and foil. When they are completely cold, store them in a cool dry place for up to 1 year.

To reheat the puddings, steam them in a covered pan of boiling water for 2½ hours.

Serves 8

Frozen Cranberry Cheese

75 g (3 oz) thick honey

2 tablespoons water

175 g (6 oz) fresh or frozen cranberries

375 g (12 oz) low fat soft cheese

150 ml (¼ pint) soured cream

3 tablespoons rosehip syrup

1 tablespoon orange juice

mint leaves, to decorate

Sauce:

2 tablespoons thick honey

2 tablespoons water

2 tablespoons orange juice

175 g (6 oz) fresh or frozen cranberries

1 teaspoon cornflour

Melt the honey in the water. Add the cranberries and simmer for 10 minutes until tender. Leave to cool.

Purée the fruit in a blender and press through a sieve.

Beat together the cheese and soured cream. Gradually beat in the fruit purée, the rosehip syrup and orange juice until smooth — or use a food processor.

Transfer the mixture to a 900 ml (1½ pint) mould. Cover with foil and freeze for 4 hours.

To make the sauce, melt the honey in the water and orange juice. Add the cranberries and simmer for 5 minutes. Do not allow them to break up. Pour a little of the juice into the cornflour and mix to make a smooth paste. Add the mixture to the fruit and stir gently over a low heat for 4–5 minutes until the sauce thickens and becomes transparent. Cool.

Unmould the dessert and leave it in the refrigerator for 1¼ hours to soften. Decorate with mint leaves. Serve the sauce separately.

Serves 6

Strawberry Wine Syllabub

300 ml (½ pint) Greek yogurt
2 teaspoons orange rind
1 tablespoon orange juice
50 g (2 oz) soft light brown sugar
100 ml (3½ fl oz) rosé wine
500 g (1 lb) strawberries, halved if large

Beat the yogurt with the orange rind and orange juice. Beat in the sugar, then gradually pour on the wine, beating all the time. Chill in

top left: Christmas pudding
left: frozen cranberry cheese, strawberry wine syllabub
right: brown sugar meringues with bramble sauce

the refrigerator for at least 1 hour. Reserve a few strawberries for the decoration, then lightly stir the remainder into the syllabub.

Pour the dessert into a bowl or 6 individual glasses and decorate with the reserved strawberries.

Serves 6

Brown Sugar Meringues with Bramble Sauce

2 egg whites
2 drops lemon juice
125 g (4 oz) soft light brown sugar
1 teaspoon cornflour
½ teaspoon vanilla essence
250 g (8 oz) low fat soft cheese
Sauce:
2 cooking apples, peeled, cored and chopped
150 ml (¼ pint) sweet cider
375 g (12 oz) blackberries
2 tablespoons cassis sirop (optional)

Line 2 baking sheets with nonstick baking paper. Whisk the egg whites with the lemon juice until they stand in peaks. Add half the sugar and whisk until stiff and glossy. Fold in the rest of the sugar with the cornflour and vanilla essence.

Using a piping bag and medium star nozzle, pipe 8 thick 'S' shapes and 8 swirls of meringue on to the baking paper.

Bake in a preheated oven, 120°C (250°F), Gas Mark ½, for 1½ hours until firm on the surface, changing the baking sheets from higher to lower shelves after 45 minutes.

Peel the meringues from the paper and place them upside-down on the baking sheets.

Return the meringues to the oven for 1 hour to dry completely.

Cool the meringues on a wire rack. When they are cold, store them in an airtight tin.

To make the sauce, simmer the apples in the cider until they are tender. Liquidize them in a blender. Return to the pan, then add the blackberries and sirop, if using. Simmer for 5 minutes. Serve the sauce hot or cold.

Just before serving, sandwich the meringues together in pairs with the low fat soft cheese. Serve the sauce separately.

Serves 4

Mint Ice Folds

75 g (3 oz) soft light brown sugar

150 ml (¼ pint) water

50 g (2 oz) mint leaves

2 tablespoons lemon juice

300 ml (½ pint) natural yogurt

mint sprigs, to decorate

Sauce:

2 cooking apples, peeled, cored and
  chopped

2 tablespoons water

3 tablespoons crème de menthe
  liqueur

2 tablespoons clear honey

2 tablespoons lemon juice

Put the sugar and water into a pan and stir over low heat to dissolve the sugar. Add the mint leaves, bring to the boil and simmer for 5 minutes. Remove from the heat and leave the syrup until it is completely cold.

Strain the mint leaves, pressing them against the sieve to extract all the moisture and flavour.

Stir the lemon juice into the cold syrup, then pour it into the yogurt, beating constantly.

Pour the mixture into a container, cover with foil and freeze for 1 hour. Turn the partly frozen mixture into a chilled bowl and beat it thoroughly to break down the ice crystals. Return the mixture to the freezer for 3–4 hours until it is really firm.

To make the sauce, simmer the apples in the water until they are mushy. Beat them well or purée

them in a blender, then stir in the liqueur, honey and lemon juice. Simmer for 3–4 minutes, stirring frequently. Leave to cool.

Transfer the pudding to the refrigerator for 30 minutes to soften. Scoop it from the container with a tablespoon and arrange the 'folds' on a dish. Decorate with mint sprigs. Serve the sauce separately.

Serves 4

Red Fruit Salad

750 g (1½ lb) raspberries

4 tablespoons clear honey

250 g (8 oz) dessert cherries, pitted

250 g (8 oz) blackcurrants, stripped
  from stalks

Curd Cheese:

¾ teaspoon powdered agar agar

2 tablespoons hot water

375 g (12 oz) cottage cheese, sieved

150 ml (¼ pint) natural yogurt

4 tablespoons double cream

grated nutmeg, to decorate

To make the curd cheese, soak the agar agar in the water in a pan for 5 minutes. Heat until dissolved, then boil for 2–3 minutes, stirring.

Beat together the cottage cheese, yogurt and cream, then stir in the agar agar.

Spoon the mixture into 4 draining moulds or yogurt pots. If using yogurt pots, cover them with muslin and invert them to drain over a dish. Leave overnight.

Purée half the raspberries, then press through a sieve into a pan. Stir the honey into the purée. Add the remaining raspberries, the cherries and blackcurrants and simmer over a low heat for 2–3 minutes. Cool, then chill for at least 1 hour.

Turn out the curd cheese moulds and decorate them with a pinch of grated nutmeg. Serve them with the fruit salad as a substantial 'sauce'.

Serves 4

Corinth Pancakes

125 g (4 oz) wholemeal flour

1 egg, beaten

150 ml (¼ pint) unsweetened orange
  juice

150 ml (¼ pint) soda water

salt

oil or fat, for frying

demerara sugar, for sprinkling

Filling:

250 g (8 oz) low fat soft cheese

150 ml (¼ pint) natural yogurt

1 tablespoon lemon rind

2 teaspoons lemon juice

125 g (4 oz) currants

50 g (2 oz) dried stoned dates,
  chopped

Mix together the flour and salt and beat in the egg. Gradually beat in the orange juice and soda water.

Use the minimum of oil or fat to grease a 20 cm (8 inch) omelette

pan. When the pan is hot, pour in enough of the batter to cover the base with a thin film. Cook until the pancake is brown and bubbling on the underside. Flip or toss and cook the other side.

Keep the cooked pancakes warm while you make the remaining ones in the same way.

To make the filling, beat together the soft cheese, yogurt, lemon rind and lemon juice, then stir in the currants and dates.

Spread some of the mixture over each pancake. Fold each one in half, then in half again, so that they are wedge shaped.

Arrange the pancakes in a heated flameproof dish. Sprinkle the demerara sugar over the pancakes and cook them under a preheated moderate grill for about 3–4 minutes until the sugar topping caramelizes. Serve immediately.

Makes 8 pancakes

above: mint ice folds, red fruit salad, Corinth pancakes

Cakes and Breads

Moist Carrot and Walnut Cake

175 ml (6 fl oz) vegetable oil

250 g (8 oz) light soft brown sugar

2 eggs

125 g (4 oz) plain wholemeal flour, sifted

1 teaspoon ground cinnamon

1 teaspoon bicarbonate of soda

150 g (5 oz) coarsely grated carrots

50 g (2 oz) chopped walnuts

Topping:

2 tablespoons apricot jam

1 tablespoon lemon juice

50 g (2 oz) chopped walnuts

Line an 18 cm (7 inch) fixed-base round cake tin with nonstick baking paper or greased greaseproof paper.

Gradually whisk the oil into the sugar. Whisk in the eggs, 1 at a time.

Mix together the flour, cinnamon and bicarbonate of soda and add to the egg mixture with the carrots and walnuts. Beat together with a wooden spoon, then pour the mixture into the prepared tin.

Bake in a preheated oven, 180°C (350°F), Gas Mark 4, for about 1¼ hours until risen and firm to the touch. Cool in the tin for 3 minutes, then peel off the paper and cool on a wire rack.

To make the topping, boil the jam and lemon juice in a small pan for 2–3 minutes. Brush generously over the top of the cake and immediately sprinkle the walnuts over.

Makes 1 x 18 cm (7 inch) round cake

Little Marzipan and Apple Pies

Pastry:

375 g (12 oz) wholemeal self-raising flour

pinch of salt

250 g (8 oz) hard vegetable margarine, from the freezer

scant 7 tablespoons water

2 tablespoons vegetable oil

Filling:

300 g (10 oz) Bramley apples, peeled, cored and coarsely chopped

125 g (4 oz) bought marzipan, cut into 5 mm (¼ inch) cubes

milk for brushing

1 tablespoon demerara sugar (optional)

To make the pastry, put the flour and salt into a bowl. Grate the margarine straight into the flour, dipping the grater into the bowl now and again to free the flakes of margarine. Distribute the margarine gently through the flour, using a round-bladed knife, then add the water and oil. Mix to a fairly firm dough, then place in a polythene bag and chill in the refrigerator for 1 hour if possible.

To make the filling, mix the apples and marzipan in a bowl.

Roll out the pastry quite thinly on a lightly floured surface. Cut out 40 rounds, using a 7 cm (3 inch) fluted cutter. Line 20 small tartlet tins with half the rounds, and spoon the filling into them, packing it well in. Brush both sides of the remaining rounds with milk and lay them on top of the tartlets in the tins. Press the edges together to seal and sprinkle each one with a little demerara sugar, if liked.

Bake near the top of a preheated oven, 220°C (425°F), Gas Mark 7, for 15–20 minutes until golden.

Carefully lift the pies from the tins and leave to cool slightly on a wire rack. Serve warm or cold.

Makes 20 pies

right: moist carrot and walnut cake, little marzipan and apple pies

Fruity Bars

So easy to make, these fruity petit fours are delicious with coffee. Cut into slices they would make a special treat for a packed lunch.

175 g (6 oz) best quality ready-to-eat
   dried apricots, finely chopped
50 g (2 oz) seedless raisins, finely
   chopped
50 g (2 oz) pecan nuts, finely
   chopped
50 g (2 oz) ground hazelnuts

grated rind of 1 orange
2 dessertspoons clear honey
about 2 dessertspoons lemon juice
icing sugar, for dusting

Combine the apricots, raisins, pecan nuts, hazelnuts and orange rind in a small bowl. Mix in all the honey and 1 dessertspoon of the lemon juice. Stir in the remaining lemon juice gradually until the mixture is a firm paste.

Turn the mixture on to a piece of baking foil and pat into an oblong shape, about 1.5 cm (¾ inch) thick.

Wrap the foil round to make a flat packet and refrigerate for about 3 hours until firm.

Remove the foil and cut the fruit and nut bar with a sharp knife into small pieces, about 1 cm (½ inch) wide and 3.5 cm (1½ inches) long.

Dust lightly with a little icing sugar before serving.

Makes about 375 g (12 oz)

below: fruity bars,
lemon and almond cake
right: apricot cake

Lemon and Almond Cake

The sharp lemon syrup spooned over the hot upside-down cake gives a distinctive flavour. The cake keeps very well for up to 1 week.

25 g (1 oz) flaked almonds
125 g (4 oz) soft vegetable margarine
125 g (4 oz) soft light brown sugar
2 eggs, beaten
grated rind of 1 lemon
125 g (4 oz) wholemeal self-raising flour, sifted
Syrup:
75 g (3 oz) caster sugar
3–4 tablespoons lemon juice

Line the base of a round 23 cm (9 inch) sandwich tin with nonstick baking paper or greased greaseproof paper. Thoroughly grease the sides of the tin. Tip the almonds into the tin and shake them around so that they cling to the sides and base.

Put the margarine and sugar into a bowl and cream them together until light and fluffy. Gradually beat in the eggs, 1 tablespoon at a time, then beat in the lemon rind. Fold in the flour until smoothly blended, then spoon the mixture into the prepared tin. Smooth the top.

Bake the cake near the centre of a preheated oven, 180°C (350°F), Gas Mark 4, for 20–25 minutes until risen and firm to the touch.

Meanwhile, make the syrup. Put the caster sugar into a small bowl and stir in the lemon juice. Leave to stand, stirring occasionally.

When the cake is cooked, remove from the oven and leave in the tin for 1 minute, then turn out upside-down on to a wire rack and carefully peel off the lining paper.

Spoon the lemon syrup evenly over the hot cake, covering the nuts, allowing it to soak in. Allow to cool, then serve cut into slices.

Makes 1 x 23 cm (9 inch) cake

Apricot Cake

125 g (4 oz) soft margarine
125 g (4 oz) soft light brown sugar
2 large eggs, beaten
200 g (7 oz) wholemeal self-raising flour
½ teaspoon baking powder
½ teaspoon ground cinnamon
250 g (8 oz) ready-to-eat dried apricots, chopped
125 g (4 oz) seedless raisins
2 tablespoons demerara sugar
Topping:
125 g (4 oz) ready-to-eat dried apricots
150 ml (¼ pint) soured cream
1 tablespoon clear honey
2 tablespoons blanched almonds, toasted and chopped

Grease and line an 18 cm (7 inch) cake tin.

Beat the margarine and sugar together until it is light and fluffy, then gradually beat in the eggs. Sift the flour, baking powder and cinnamon and tip in any bran left in the sieve. Gradually add the dry ingredients to the creamed mixture. Stir in the apricots and raisins and beat well.

Turn the mixture into the prepared cake tin, level the top and sprinkle on the demerara sugar.

Bake in a preheated oven, 160°C (325°F), Gas Mark 3, for 1½ hours or until a skewer pierced through the centre of the cake comes out clean.

Stand the cake in the tin on a wire rack to cool. Then peel off the paper and leave the cake to become completely cool.

Purée the apricots in a blender and beat in the soured cream and honey. Spread the topping over the cake. Sprinkle the chopped nuts around the edge, to decorate.

Makes 1 x 18 cm (7 inch) cake

Carob Honey Cake

75 g (3 oz) soft light brown sugar

175 g (6 oz) clear honey

50 g (2 oz) wholemeal flour

3 tablespoons carob powder

½ teaspoon ground cinnamon

25 g (1 oz) ground almonds

1 tablespoon grated orange rind

50 g (2 oz) candied orange peel, chopped

175 g (6 oz) hazelnuts

125 g (4 oz) blanched almonds, lightly toasted

Grease and flour a 20 cm (8 inch) flan ring on a baking sheet or a loose-bottomed cake tin.

Melt the sugar and honey over a low heat, then simmer, stirring frequently, for 10 minutes.

Sift the flour, carob powder and cinnamon, tip in any bran left in the sieve and stir in the ground almonds and orange rind. Pour on the honey mixture, stir quickly, then stir in the peel and nuts. Beat thoroughly.

Spread the mixture into the flan ring or tin and bake in a preheated oven, 140°C (275°F), Gas Mark 1, for 30 minutes until firm.

Cool the cake in the flan ring or tin on a wire rack.

Makes 1 x 20 cm (8 inch) cake

Celebration Fruit Cake

200 g (7 oz) dried stoned dates, finely chopped

150 ml (¼ pint) milk, plus extra if needed (see method)

125 g (4 oz) soft margarine

3 eggs, beaten

250 g (8 oz) wholemeal flour

2 teaspoons baking powder

1 teaspoon ground cinnamon

½ teaspoon ground ginger

large pinch of grated nutmeg

2 teaspoons grated orange rind

1 tablespoon orange juice

50 g (2 oz) ground almonds

50 g (2 oz) blanched almonds, chopped

250 g (8 oz) seedless raisins

175 g (6 oz) currants

50 g (2 oz) sultanas

50 g (2 oz) candied orange peel, chopped

Apricot Paste:

125 g (4 oz) blanched almonds

250 g (8 oz) ready-to-eat dried apricots, chopped

2 tablespoons soft light brown sugar

1 tablespoon lemon juice

1 tablespoon clear honey, warmed

Grease a 20 cm (8 inch) cake tin and line with greased greaseproof paper.

Mash the dates with the milk and heat them over a very low heat, stirring constantly, until they form

a thick paste. Set aside to cool, then beat with the margarine. Gradually beat in the eggs.

Sift the flour, baking powder and spices. Add any bran left in the sieve and the orange rind.

Gradually add the dry ingredients to the date mixture, beating all the time. Beat in the orange juice, ground and chopped almonds, raisins, currants, sultanas and peel. Add a little milk if necessary to give a firm dropping consistency.

Turn the mixture into the tin and level the top. Bake in a preheated oven, 150°C (300°F), Gas Mark 2, for 2 ¾–3 hours until a fine skewer pierced into the centre of the cake comes out clean.

Leave the cake in the tin and stand it on a wire rack to cool.

To make the apricot paste, grind or chop the almonds until they are as fine as semolina. Reserve 2 teaspoons of the ground almonds, then add the apricots, sugar and lemon juice and process to a smooth paste. Knead the paste on a board lightly sprinkled with the remaining ground almonds.

Roll out the paste to a thickness of 5 mm (¼ inch) and cut out decorative shapes and a thick band to cover the side of the cake. Brush the side of the cake with the honey and press on the strip of apricot paste. Brush the decoration for the top with honey and press on to the top of the cake. Close-wrap the cake in foil and store it in an airtight tin.

Makes 1 x 20 cm (8 inch) cake

Note: The apricot paste can be made in advance, wrapped in foil and stored in an airtight container. Store the cut-out shapes stacked between layers of greaseproof paper or polythene.

Honey Spice Ring

150 g (5 oz) soft margarine
50 g (2 oz) soft light brown sugar
3 tablespoons clear honey
2 eggs, beaten
175 g (6 oz) wholemeal self-raising flour
1½ teaspoons mixed ground spice
½ teaspoon ground ginger
75 g (3 oz) walnuts, chopped
Filling:
250 g (8 oz) cottage cheese, sieved
150 ml (¼ pint) natural yogurt
50 g (2 oz) soft light brown sugar
50 g (2 oz) candied orange peel, chopped
50 g (2 oz) seedless raisins
25 g (1 oz) blanched almonds, chopped
1 tablespoon grated orange rind

Grease and flour a 1 litre (1¾ pint) ring mould.

Make the filling the day before. Beat the cheese, yogurt and sugar. Stir in the peel, raisins, almonds and orange rind and beat well.

Line a sieve with a double layer of scalded muslin. Spoon in the cheese filling, cover it with muslin and put a plate and heavy weight on top. Leave the cheese to drain overnight.

To make the cake, cream the margarine, sugar and honey until the mixture is light and fluffy. Stir in the eggs. Sift the flour and spices and tip in any bran left in the sieve. Fold the flour into the creamed mixture and stir in the walnuts.

Spoon the mixture into the prepared mould. Stand the mould on a baking sheet and bake in a preheated oven, 180°C (350°F), Gas Mark 4, for 40 minutes until the cake is well risen.

Leave the cake to cool in the mould, then turn it out on to a wire rack and leave until cold.

Turn the cake on to a serving dish. Fork over the cheese filling and spoon some into the centre of the ring.

Makes 1 x 1 litre (1¾ pint) ring cake

Variation:
The cheese filling is a simple adaptation of the Russian Easter dessert known as pashka. It is also delicious served with fresh or simmered soft fruits.

left: celebration fruit cake, honey spice ring

Mixed Fruit Loaf

This quickly made loaf is a cross between bread and cake, crusty outside and moist inside. It is equally delicious plain, or spread with unsalted butter. The loaf keeps well in an airtight tin for up to 1 week.

75 g (3 oz) sultanas

50 g (2 oz) raisins

50 g (2 oz) currants

25 g (1 oz) ready-to-eat dried apricots, finely chopped

75 g (3 oz) light soft brown sugar

grated rind of 1 lemon

¼ teaspoon ground cinnamon

pinch of grated nutmeg

50 ml (2 fl oz) unsweetened orange juice

1 egg, beaten

2 tablespoons vegetable oil

175 g (6 oz) wholemeal self-raising flour

Line a 500 g (1 lb) loaf tin with nonstick baking paper or greased greaseproof paper.

Put the sultanas, raisins, currants and apricots into a bowl and add the sugar, lemon rind, cinnamon and nutmeg.

Pour over the orange juice and stir well. Cover and leave the fruits to soak in the juice for 2 hours.

Beat in the egg and the oil and then stir in the flour. Spoon the mixture into the tin and bake in the centre of a preheated oven, 160°C (325°F), Gas Mark 3, for 50–60 minutes.

Turn out on to a wire rack, peel off the paper and leave to cool completely before slicing.

Makes 1 x 500 g (1 lb) loaf

Scone Ring with Soft Cheese and Fruit

The addition of a little oil to the scone mixture will keep the scones soft, and leaving them to rest in a warm place before baking will make them exceptionally light.

125 g (4 oz) wholemeal self-raising flour

125 g (4 oz) white self-raising flour

25 g (1 oz) light soft brown sugar

50 g (2 oz) hard vegetable margarine

125 ml (4 fl oz) milk

1 tablespoon vegetable oil

pinch of salt

milk, for brushing

To serve:

125 g–175 g (4–6 oz) curd or cream cheese

seasonal fruits (raspberries, blackberries, strawberries or peaches)

Flour a baking sheet. Mix the flours, salt and sugar in a bowl. Add the margarine and rub in until the mixture resembles breadcrumbs.

Make a well in the centre of the mixture and pour in all the milk and oil, mixing lightly with a round-bladed knife to produce a soft but not sticky consistency.

above: mixed fruit loaf
right: scone ring with soft cheese and fruit, caraway and coriander biscuists

Turn out on to a lightly floured surface and roll out 1.5 cm (¾ inch) thick. Cut out 8 scones using a 6 cm (2½ inch) round fluted cutter.

Arrange the scones in a ring, just touching, on the baking sheet. Brush with milk and leave in a warm place for 15 minutes.

Bake near the top of a preheated oven, 220°C (425°F), Gas Mark 7, for 15 minutes until well risen. Cool on a wire rack, reshaping the circle if the scones separate.

To serve, place the curd or cream cheese in a small dish in the centre of the scone ring and serve with fresh seasonal fruits.

Makes 8 scones

Caraway and Coriander Biscuits

These crisp little oat biscuits have a distinctive flavour and are quick to make. Nice with morning coffee.

200 g (7 oz) wholemeal self-raising flour
50 g (2 oz) coarse oatmeal
50 g (2 oz) soft light brown sugar
2 teaspoons ground coriander
1 teaspoon caraway seeds
175 g (6 oz) butter, at room temperature

Lightly grease a baking sheet. Put the flour, oatmeal, sugar, coriander and caraway seeds into a bowl. Cut the butter into small pieces and add to the bowl.

Using your hands, knead the mixture into a firm dough.

Roll out on a lightly floured surface to about 5 mm (¼ inch) thick. Cut out rounds using a 5 cm (2 inch) plain biscuit cutter. Gather up the trimmings, roll out again and cut out more rounds.

Arrange on the baking sheet and bake near the top of a preheated oven, 160°C (325°F), Gas Mark 3, for 20 minutes until pale brown.

Makes about 20

Fennel
Rye Bread

175 g (6 oz) strong wholemeal flour
175 g (6 oz) rye flour
½ teaspoon salt
1 teaspoon baking powder
40 g (1½ oz) soft margarine
150 ml (¼ pint) soured cream
1 egg
milk, for brushing
1 tablespoon fennel seeds

Grease a baking sheet. Sift together the flours, salt and baking powder and tip in any bran remaining in the sieve. Rub in the margarine. Beat together the soured cream and egg and stir into the dry ingredients to form a firm dough.

Knead the dough on a lightly floured board until smooth. Shape it into a round and place it on the baking sheet. Brush the top of the loaf with milk and sprinkle on the fennel seeds.

Bake in a preheated oven, 200°C (400°F), Gas Mark 6, for 1¼ hours or until the bread sounds hollow when tapped underneath. Transfer it to a wire rack to cool.

Makes 1 x 500 g (1 lb) loaf

Note: This bread is best eaten within 1 day of baking.

above: spiced pumpkin bread, fennel rye bread, Banchory muffins

Spiced Pumpkin Bread

500 g (1 lb) slice of pumpkin, peeled,
   deseeded and chopped
500 g (1 lb) wholemeal flour
½ teaspoon salt
½ teaspoon ground ginger
½ teaspoon ground cinnamon
a pinch of grated nutmeg
1 sachet easy-blend yeast
150 ml (¼ pint) tepid milk
1 egg, beaten, to glaze
2 tablespoons chopped blanched
   almonds

Steam the pumpkin over boiling water for 25–30 minutes until it is soft. Press it through a sieve or liquidize it in a blender to make a purée. Set aside to cool slightly.

Sift the flour, salt, ginger, cinnamon and nutmeg and tip in any bran remaining in the sieve. Stir in the easy-blend yeast. Beat in the pumpkin purée and milk and mix to a firm dough.

Knead the dough on a lightly floured surface until it is smooth and elastic – about 10 minutes if you are working by hand.

Place the dough in an oiled polythene bag and leave in a warm place for about 1 hour until it has doubled in size.

Knead the dough again for 5 minutes. Divide it into 2 pieces, one twice the size of the other. Put the smaller piece on the larger portion. Press the greased handle of a wooden spoon down through the centre, to join the 2 pieces of dough together.

Place the dough on a baking sheet, cover and leave in a warm place to rise for 20–25 minutes.

Brush the loaf with beaten egg and scatter the almonds on top.

Bake the loaf in a preheated oven, 200°C (400°F), Gas Mark 6, for about 55–60 minutes until it sounds hollow when tapped. Leave to cool on a wire rack.

Makes 1 x 1 kg (2 lb) loaf

Banchory Muffins

125 g (4 oz) wholemeal self-raising
   flour
2 teaspoons baking powder
salt
75 g (3 oz) medium oatmeal
40 g (1½ oz) soft light brown
   sugar
75 g (3 oz) dried stoned dates,
   chopped
1 tablespoon set honey
15 g (½ oz) soft margarine
150 ml (¼ pint) buttermilk

Grease 12 deep patty tins. In a mixing bowl, thoroughly mix together the wholemeal flour, baking powder, salt, oatmeal, brown sugar and dates .

Gently melt the honey, margarine and buttermilk in a small saucepan over a low heat, stirring, then allow to cool slightly.

Pour the milk mixture on to the dry ingredients and stir quickly to form a smooth batter.

Spoon the muffin batter into the patty tins, so that it comes just over halfway up them.

Bake the muffin mixture in a preheated oven, 200°C (400°F), Gas Mark 6, for 15–18 minutes until the muffins are well risen and firm.

Leave them to cool in the tins for 1–2 minutes, then remove the muffins from the tins and turn them out on to on a wire rack to cool. When the muffins are completely cold, store them in an airtight tin.

Makes about 12 muffins

Banana and Yogurt Teabread

50 g (2 oz) soft margarine
100 g (3½ oz) soft light brown
  sugar
1 egg, beaten
125 g (4 oz) wholemeal flour
1 large banana, about 150 g (5 oz)
2 tablespoons natural yogurt
50 g (2 oz) sultanas
2 tablespoons sunflower seeds
salt

Grease and flour a cleaned 825 g (29 oz) food can with the top removed or a 20 x 10 cm (8 x 4 inch) loaf tin.

Cream the margarine and sugar until they are light and fluffy, then beat in the egg.

Sift the flour and salt and tip in any bran left in the sieve. Mash the banana with the yogurt.

Add the flour mixture and the banana alternately to the creamed fat, beating well between each addition. Stir in the sultanas and sunflower seeds.

Spoon the mixture into the prepared can or loaf tin. Bake in a preheated oven, 160°C (325°F), Gas Mark 3, for 1–1¼ hours until the loaf is cooked. Test it by piercing the centre with a fine skewer.

Makes 1 x 'barrel' loaf or 1 x small loaf just under 500 g (1 lb)

Herb Scones

250 g (8 oz) wholemeal flour
½ teaspoon bicarbonate of soda
½ teaspoon salt
40 g (1½ oz) white vegetable fat
1 teaspoon dried oregano
½ teaspoon dried basil
75 g (3 oz) Gouda cheese, grated
150 ml (¼ pint) buttermilk
1 tablespoon tomato purée
milk, for brushing

Grease a baking sheet. Sift the flour, bicarbonate of soda and salt and rub in the fat until the mixture is like fine breadcrumbs. Stir in the dried herbs and half the cheese. Gradually stir the milk into the tomato purée so that it is well blended. Pour the mixture on to the dry ingredients and mix to form a firm dough.

Roll out the dough on a lightly floured surface to a thickness of about 1.5 cm (¾ inch).

Using a 5 cm (2 inch) cutter, cut out some rounds of the dough. Gather up the dough trimmings into a ball, roll them out again and cut more rounds.

Place the scone rounds on the baking sheet and sprinkle them with the remaining cheese.

Bake the scones in a preheated oven, 200°C (400°F), Gas Mark 6, for 20 minutes or until the scones are well risen and springy to the touch. Transfer them to a wire rack to cool.

Makes about 8–10 scones

Note: If you cannot obtain buttermilk — which, like yogurt, gives the necessary acid and the characteristic flavour to scones of all kinds — you can substitute some milk which has been soured with a little lemon juice.

Ayrshire Pan Scones

250 g (8 oz) strong wholemeal flour
1 teaspoon bicarbonate of soda
1 teaspoon salt
1 teaspoon cream of tartar
25 g (1 oz) soft margarine
15 g (½ oz) soft light brown sugar
150 ml (¼ pint) natural yogurt
100 ml (3½ fl oz) soured cream
oil, for brushing

Sift the flour, bicarbonate of soda, salt and cream of tartar and tip in any bran remaining in the sieve. Rub in the margarine and stir in the sugar. Stir in the yogurt and soured cream. Shape the mixture into a dough and knead it lightly.

Divide the dough into 2 equal pieces and shape each piece into a round. Flatten the pieces until they are 1.5 cm (¾ inch) thick.

Heat a heavy-based frying pan and very lightly brush it with oil.

Cook one scone over a moderate heat for 6–7 minutes until it is well browned on the underside. Flip it over and cook the other side. Transfer the scone to a wire rack to cool. Cook the remaining dough in the same way. Serve the scones cut into wedges.

Makes 12 scones

far left: banana and yogurt teabread
left: herb scones
above Ayrshire pan scones

Index